The New Light

A Heathen's Guide
to
Drug Addiction and Recovery

Hrafn Rekkr

Rights and Dedications

Mighty heils to Calvin Myers, WrenVillage Outreach and all who contributed to this project.

If you notice any errors, consider: This entire book was thumb-typed into a tablet roughly the size of a cheap cellphone in native HTML, constructed from *numerous* offender emails sent through JPay and compiled by a 79-year-old lady on a computer assembled from discount parts by a goat farmer, with all free software. If you can do better, do it.

Hrafn Rekkr is the heathen name of David Hemmingsen, #1412271 who is currently incarcerated in the Virginia Prison System. He has been practicing Ásatrú since 2012. He likes to get mail, so if you want to write him, look him up.

Cover art is by Christopher Todd Younger a.k.a. "Tex" #1201514, also housed in the Virginia Prison System. Get in touch and buy some artwork.

This book is still a work in progress. Future editions are expected to include a Glossary for Non-Heathens, a Bibliography, an Appendix, and even more Sagas of modern heathens and their battles with drugs. If you have something to contribute, contact the author and you might see it in the next version!

Introduction

The purpose of this book is to transform your thinking about drug addiction. It's also to show how living an Ásatrú-based lifestyle is conducive to getting and staying clean. You'll benefit from this book if you're ready for change and strive to embody the virtues of our ancestors. Alternately, it can help anyone who has a friend or loved one who suffers from addiction, or the kindred leader who wants to heal his folk.

For the person who has stumbled across this book and has never heard of Ásatrú, it is the organic religion of the Northern European people. Towards the end of the Viking age, Christian missionaries set out on a violent campaign to forcibly convert all pagan religions. Many aspects of Ásatrú went underground to avoid persecution or were absorbed in Christian traditions to placate the Northern people. While the depth of history and beauty of these ancestral ways are beyond the scope of this book, I hope that at the very least my words can inspire someone to further study.

As you set out on this path, it's enough to know that we as Ásatrúar approach everything from a position of power and personal responsibility. Submission and victim mentality run counter to our beliefs. If you are in the habit of placing the blame of your addiction on others, this may be a difficult mindset to adopt. However, if you show perseverance, then it can become the most liberating experience of your life. Along the way we will attack addiction from a scientific and cultural point of view, even as we examine the lore for any wisdom our ancestors have to offer. Also throughout the book I'll describe some of my experiences as a prison Ásatrúar and goði. By reading and applying the lessons within, you'll be fully equipped to fight (and win) your own personal war against drugs. From there you can move on to complete self-mastery.

How This Book Came About

When I became the goði of the Seeds of Oak Hofguild it was a learning experience. In many ways I couldn't have been luckier. The goði before me had done a great job of screening for niðingrs. I was surrounded by a solid group of men who were knowledgeable about our lore and way of life. Nearly any one of them could have held my position.

But there was one problem that I saw. The drug use had gotten out of control. As an Odinist I am firmly against drug use and have a clear vision of how I feel a Hammer Bearer should carry himself. Yet it seemed like every other day I was resolving disputes that stemmed from drugs. Given enough time I knew it would tear the community apart. I had seen the same thing happen in the neighborhood I grew up in.

At first I had it in my head to clean up all drug use within the community, even if it meant snatching Hammers. But in the end, I couldn't do it. Maybe I should have, but these were my brothers, men I had built frith with over the years. I knew any one of them would fight beside me without hesitation. Not to mention some of the men who had sacrificed the most for our Hofguild had struggled with addiction.

So instead of taking such drastic measures, I decided to try my best to help them overcome their addictions. That way, even if I failed, at least I could say I tried. I started with what I felt was a small step: No dealing drugs within the community. To say this was an unpopular decision would be an understatement. But even though my brothers didn't like the decision, they had enough respect for me to follow it.

Well, most of them did. I expected someone to try me and I wasn't disappointed. I won't go into any details, but one guy went against the grain. I told my Logmaðr and we pulled up on him at the next group meeting. To his credit, he didn't try to deny it. At that point it was about finding a suitable wergild.

My Logmaðr at the time was the man who had first sponsored me for a Hammer years ago. There's no one whom I respect more. That being said, I didn't agree with his decision back then. He suggested that we make our brother design a recovery program for heathens.

Let's just say I thought he was getting off lightly.

The book you're holding in your hands shows whose idea we took. The rough draft of that recovery program grew into this one. And the more time that passes, the more certain I am that we made the right decision. Bruises and black eyes fade, but hopefully this book leaves a legacy of helping those Ásatrúar who struggle with addiction.

The New Light

The title of this book comes from a story in the Ásatrú Edda that I like to teach which perfectly illustrates the effects of corruption on a community.

It all started in the Silver Age when Gullveig, a beautiful Jötun hostage, began to plot her revenge on the Goðin. She knew that the Æsir were far too powerful to attack directly, so she used cunning to defile what they held dear; the pure men and women of Midgard whom Heimdall had instructed.

So she poured all her hatred into a great work and created the evil seiðr. With seiðr she could corrupt otherwise wholesome things and bring about the death, ill-luck or bad health of people. Mental aberration, mistrust, theft and murder followed in her wake.

Sound familiar?

Ásatrú is a reconstructionist religion which means we are in the process of trying to piece together the beliefs of our ancestors. But it's not enough to comb the lore for every esoteric custom or ritual if we completely ignore the spirit of these beliefs. That's why I propose that drugs are modern day seiðr. If our ancestors could witness the soul crushing aspects of addictive substances, I'm sure they would equate them with seiðr.

When Odin saw the chaos taking place in Midgard, he sent the Dís Nyhellenia-Gefjon to investigate. Her name literally meant *The New Light* and she would become a beacon of hope for the Folk. As soon as she discovered the area where all the problems seemed to originate, she made it her home and set out to discover the source.

It didn't take long before she recognized Gullveig was posing as a wise woman named Heidr. Knowing that the Jötnar are a jealous and arrogant lot, Nyhellenia began to show that she, too, was a wise woman. When the old Folkmóðir died, Gullveig and Nyhellenia were both nominated for the position.

This was too much for Gullveig. It enraged her to be compared to a young upstart and her composure began to slip. Nyhellenia, for her part, subtly antagonized the witch. Slowly, Gullveig's true nature was revealed. If the Folk wouldn't love her, then she would rule them through fear.

But first she would have to kill Nyhellenia. During a festival Gullveig poured beer with magic mixed in it. When the people were all drunk, she used poisonous words to turn them against Nyhellenia. In a drunken rage they set out to kill the noble Dis, but with the help of the Sea-Folk she managed to escape.

Once tempers cooled and the alcohol wore off, the people were relieved that they didn't commit this terrible nid and were willing to hear her out. The goðord (the priests and leaders) asked her how to best heal the community. Her advice was both wise and practical:

On evil people... There are those out there who root about in the gloom, who plan ruses, to rob people of their wits until they take hold over them so as to make slaves of them and to suck their blood like the draugr.

On why evil exists... Odin wants us to seek help and advice ourselves so that we shall become strong and wise. If we will not, then he lets us struggle out our bewilderment so that we may learn what follows after wise and after stupid deeds.

On tru leaders as role models... "The sparrows follow the sower, the people their good princes; therefore, you should begin by making yourselves pure so that you may direct your gaze, both inward and outward, without becoming ashamed of your own mind."

The people were so impressed by Nyhellenia that they elected her as Folkmóðir. Gullveig was captured by the Goðin and burned at the stake.

Our Folk are still struggling with the same problems. We may be more technologically advanced but the core of human nature is the same as it has always been. That's why the Seeds of Oak have created this program: To become a New Light for those who are stumbling in the shadow of addiction.

How to Use This Book

This book is separated into three sections: The Nine Paths, Runic Recovery, and Personal Sagas.

The Nine Paths: Similar to a 12 step program, just three steps more efficient. At the end of each chapter is the story of Matt, a man recently released from prison who's struggling to beat his addiction. While Matt's story is fictional, it's also a composite of men I've known. The paths themselves are meant to be walked one at a time, in order; however, if you're anything like me you'll read them all to get a feel for what to expect, then go back and complete the exercises. That's fine AS LONG AS YOU COMPLETE THE EXERCISES. As the saying goes, "Learning without thought is wasted effort."

Runic Recovery: These are essays on how each rune of the Elder Futhark relates to drug addiction. You can either read them straight through, or if you have a rune set, draw a rune, meditate on it, then read the essay. Remember that the runes speak to everyone differently so your UPG (unverified personal gnosis) is no less valid than anyone else's.

Personal Sagas: These are the stories of other Ásatrúar whose lives have been impacted by drugs. They can either be read alone or aloud during a hall.

May you walk with the Goðin on the road to recovery.

Ves Heil,

Seeds of Oak Hofguild

R. E. 2267

The Path of Truth

No virtue other than truth could be at the beginning of this program. Without truth, you can't find your way to the other paths, only to the blind alleys of self-delusion. It is the first step you must take, but that doesn't make it the easiest. In fact, taking a deep and honest look at yourself could be the hardest thing you've ever had to do. Most of us aren't chasing drugs, we're running from ourselves.

Hands down, the proudest I've ever been of any Ásatrúar has to be my brother Lucky. Lucky is the type of guy you would love to have by your side in a fight. In a group filled with physically fit men, he outshines us all. The Ásaman. But the pride I felt for him had nothing to do with his strength on the weight pile. It was his strength of character that impressed me. When the time came for him to don his Hammer, he seemed reluctant to make the commitment. Guys were pressuring him until he said he felt like he didn't deserve the honor yet. You see, Lucky struggled with addiction and deep down he knew what Mjöllnir represented.

Eventually Lucky made an oath to quit doing drugs and donned his Hammer. I'd love to be able to say that he has been clean to this day, but this is a chapter on truth. He made it a solid ten months before he relapsed. I'd suspected he'd started using again, but Luck's the type to keep things to himself.

That year he and I did the bare-chested workout together. For those who are unfamiliar with the barechested workout, also known as the Vinland Tradition, it's where all Ásatrúar across the state prison take their shirts off and work out in the freezing cold on Mother Night. There's a portion of the ceremony in which any participant who feels they've committed a nid can pour a cup of ice water over their head. You can tell a lot about a man during this ordeal. Maybe he doesn't admit any wrongdoing. Or maybe he pours the water

6

quickly to get it over with. Lucky told me he'd messed up. He didn't go into the details but I knew what he meant and I watched as he poured the ice water slowly over his head. I did the same and we completed the workout.

Lucky showed he was a true Ásaman by being honest about his faults. Why is it so hard for others to do the same?

The Power of Self-Delusion

Men seem to have an endless capacity to choose a beautiful lie over an ugly truth. Our ego is so fragile, yet so expert at self-preservation, that it will go to great lengths to protect itself. No one wants to be the bad guy of the story. No one wakes up every morning thinking about what piece of shit things they can do. Yet when you look around there are a lot of piece of shit things being done. How can people look themselves in the mirror and not feel like a hypocrite?

Self-delusion. Rationalization.

Here's an example. When I first made it clear that there was to be no more dealing drugs within the community, one guy in particular was upset. He tried to convince me that, by selling drugs to his bros he was actually the good guy. When they dealt with him, at least they knew what they were getting and they wouldn't get ripped off. It's the old, "They're going to get the drugs anyways, they might as well get them from me" rationalization. Forget that you're preying on a brother's weakness. Forget that in Ásatrú we believe that we are our **own** deeds, not the next man's. All that is irrelevant when the ego feels threatened and reaches for justification. Yet sadly this type of convoluted thinking is all too common with addicts.

If this drug dealer had walked the Path of Truth he would've come to a far different conclusion. He might've been able to admit that he liked the excitement of selling drugs. Or maybe he would've seen that he sold drugs so he could get high for free.

I can't count how many times I've heard someone say, "You know, I haven't even been getting high lately." They say it like they're expecting a congratulations. But what they don't know is that I'm aware that there haven't been any drugs in the prison for however long they've been sober. Not getting high is not the same as not being **able** to get high. Yet in their minds they've willingly gotten clean.

The really creative self-deceivers even find ways to justify their drug use with Ásatrú. Let me know if any of these rationalizations sound familiar...

1. *"Our ancestors were free spirits who wouldn't want anyone telling them what to do."* True, our ancestors were individualistic people who valued their freedom. They were even encouraged to exercise this freedom to the extent that it did no harm to the community. However, severe forms of punishment were reserved for those who were a drain on, or took advantage of, the Folk.

2. *"Odin promotes moderation, not abstinence."* This is one of my favorites. In the Havamal, when Odin speaks on moderation, he's talking about mead, a drink with 5-7% alcohol content. This pales in comparison to the liquor of today. It can't even be compared to hard drugs. As I've stated before, if Odin or our ancestors had come across coke, meth, heroin, or synthetics they would have viewed them as evil magic. Seidr.

3. *"Our ancestors used drugs in ritual."* While there's not a lot of hard evidence for Northern European shamanism, it's likely, judging by other pagan cultures, that drugs were used to induce altered states of consciousness. Psilocybin mushrooms are a possible candidate. That being said, the men and women who participated in these rituals were probably highly trained and supervised. And let's be honest; you're not looking for a mystical experience at the end of a rolled-up dollar bill.

Now that we've identified some of the common excuses, it's time to take the next step.

Are You an Addict?

If you use drugs, how do you know if you are addicted? This is a difficult question to answer, especially because there are so many definitions of what an addict is. Someone who's more straightedged will view any type of drug use as addict behavior. To them, there is no such thing as recreational use. At the other end of the spectrum, a person might feel it's a good week if they haven't woken up in the gutter, or pawned the family's flat screen.

As for myself, I fall more towards the straightedged side because I know how slippery a slope drug use can be for me. Also, I'm not a functional addict. Partying and recovering from partying quickly eclipse everything positive in my life. My job is the first to go because who wants to work with a hangover when its easier to sell drugs and set your own hours? My relationships and family obligations circle the toilet soon after. So it has taken some hard lessons but I've learned it's better not to get high at all.

But another lesson I've learned is that not everyone is like me. Some people can drink one beer, smoke one J, or do a single line without going on a three day binge. I've known guys who can "just party on the weekends." So how do you know if you're one of these rare people? The problem is you won't know until you do know, and then it may be too late.

For the majority of people, losing control is a gradual process. The slow development of addiction is supported by recent advances in brain physiology. Each time you use a drug, you cause a small but lasting change in your brain's functioning and circuitry. Eventually, you'll cross a threshold where the brain pathways that control impulses and decision-making are irrevocably set. You will no longer be able to resist the temptation, no matter what the other parts of the brain logically think or desire.

Does this sound like you? One of the most common ways to screen yourself for addiction is the CAGE questionnaire.

- **C:** Have you ever tried to **cut** down on your drug use?
- **A:** Are you ever **annoyed** when people mention your drug use?
- **G:** Do you ever feel **guilty** about your drug use?
- **E:** Do you ever use drugs first thing in the morning (an **"Eye-opener"**)?

If you answered yes to two or more questions, there is a very good chance that you have a substance abuse problem.

Here are some additional questions to ask yourself to help determine if your drug use is getting out of control:

- How often do you use drugs and is your drug use increasing? Think back to how often you got high a year ago. Did you start as a recreational user and either gradually or steadily increase

9

to a full time user?

- How much do you use? Do you do more or less of your drug of choice than those around you? Can you do a small amount and then set it aside, or do you often obsess about doing more? Has your tolerance increased, making it harder to get high off the same amount?
- How do you use your drug of choice? Every user knows there are more efficient ways of doing drugs, but the better the high, the more addictive. If you started snorting coke are you now smoking crack? If you started snorting heroin or meth, are you now injecting or smoking it?
- Are you doing things to get drugs that you would've never done in the past? Have you gone to dangerous places to cop drugs or dealt with shady people? Have you stolen from family or friends to support your habit? Do you consistently live counter to the nine noble virtues?
- Do you notice that your drug use determines the people you hang out with? Take a look at the people around you on a consistent basis. If they had no connections to the drug game, would they still be people you'd want to hang out with? Are there people in your life who you used to love and respect, but now seem boring and unapproachable?
- Has your health suffered because of drug use? Have you caught STDs because you were high and didn't take usual precautions? Have you experienced chest pains, panic attacks, or severe paranoia? Are you depressed?

And for those Ásatrúar who are in prison:

- Have you used drugs despite being suspected by the administration to be a user? Most prisons have a "hot sheet", a list of offenders who are known drug users. These offenders are given urinalysis tests on a regular basis. Have you been on a list like this and still used drugs, knowing its more likely that you will get caught? Do you try to "beat" the tests?
- Do you get visits from family and friends and still use drugs? Many prisons will suspend an offender's visitation privileges for a dirty urine. Do you still risk not being able to see your loved ones just to get high?
- Have you ever been so high that you couldn't help a brother if

he needed you in an altercation? Prison can be a dangerous place. For months things may run smoothly and then all of a sudden the shit hits the fan. Have you ever been nodding out or hungover when a brother needed you?

And when you're done asking yourself these questions, it's time to ask the most important question of all…

Do You Deserve to Wear Your Hammer?

I understand this is a dangerous question to ask any Ásatrúar. If someone questions my right to wear Mjöllnir, they'd better be ready to fight. It's a natural reaction since most of us have given our blood, sweat, and tears to this way of life. The path we walk is not an easy or a popular one. That being said, the Hammer represents everything that is noble within our people. The Hammer around my neck was given to me by a brother named Copper. He once said that you will never find a perfect Ásatrúar, that we're like rocks, we all have flaws to our character. The Hammer is meant to chip away at these imperfections. So while we don't expect perfection, that doesn't mean we stop trying to achieve it.

If you are a Hammer bearer, you bear a responsibility to Family, Faith, and Folk. Are you a worthy representative? If someone were to see you on the street, or on the yard, are you the type of person they would respect and want to emulate? What about the times when no one is around? As a brother of mine named Jeff likes to say, "Honor is what you do when no one's looking."

The Hammer is a symbol of all who have lived and died for it. Without that, it's just a lump of metal or wood, a fashion statement. Other generations have nearly forgotten it. We don't want to be the generation who tarnishes what it represents. That's why I'm asking anyone who feels like they don't deserve to wear Mjöllnir to set it aside for the time being, not as a punishment, but as a sign of respect. Use this time to work these paths and chip away at your imperfections. If you persevere, then one day, I promise you will be even more worthy to wear it.

Matt's Saga

Life after prison hadn't turned out the way Matt planned.

An understatement, he thought, as he pulled into the cheap motel he now called home.

"Baby, how long till he gets here?" Aaryn asked. He could feel the impatience, the **need** coming off her in waves. She was only twenty five but the bags under her blue eyes and her skeletal cheeks made her look much older. He could still remember his release day, how beautiful she'd looked. Her downward spiral was his fault, like so much else.

"Soon," Matt replied. He took a drag from his cigarette, his hands shaking. It wasn't supposed to be like this. He'd had such high hopes. A job lined up. A woman who loved him and stood by him. No way he was gonna fuck that up and become another recidivist statistic. Yet here he was, out here in the streets, chasing again.

Streetlight gleamed off the tarnished Hammer around his neck, and, not for the first time, he wondered what his brothers back in prison would have to say about his choices. Like always, the thought carried the shame of broken promises.

These thoughts were interrupted when a pearl Navigator pulled up. His dealer, a guy named Q., climbed out and stuck his head in Matt's window. His dreds smelled like stale blunts.

"What're you looking for?" Q. asked.

"The usual. A ball.""

"You know what it is."

"Alright. Thing is, I can't get you until Monday."

"Aww, hell no. You called me out here and you ain't got no money?"

"You know I'm good for it," Matt said, hating the whiny tone of his voice. "I'll cash my check Monday morning."

"Fuck that. You still owe me fifty. Why don't you give me that chain and I'll throw you a half gram?"

Matt looked down at his Hammer again and thought of all that he'd gone through to earn it. Even so, it took everything in him to say it wasn't for sale.

Q. shrugged and looked Aaryn up and down. "What about your girl? She try'n to party? I'll make it worth both your while."

Aaryn looked to Matt to say something, but he hesitated. He was torn. A part of him wanted to kill this dude for disrespecting her. But another part of him just wanted a blast.

Taking Matt's silence as a yes, Q. tossed a baggie in his lap. "Don't worry… I'm gonna treat her real good."

Matt watched in a daze as Q. led Aaryn to their hotel room. He could see her hand was trembling as she tried to swipe the key card. It took a few tries for the door to open. When it did, she shot him one last scared look before it closed behind her.

That look was what finally brought him to his senses. What was he doing? This was Aaryn. The woman he'd been with since high school. The only one who'd stood beside him during his prison bid. And here he was about to trade her for a few hits of crack.

He'd always wondered what rock bottom felt like. Now he knew. He grabbed the tire iron from beneath the seat and headed for the door.

Matt burst into the room. Q. spilled the drink he was fixing for Aaryn, who was perched on the edge of the bed. Thank the Goðin nothing had happened yet.

"What the hell are you doing? We had a deal."

"Get out. Now." Matt threw the baggie and it bounced off Q.'s chest.

"You're gonna regret this."

"Not as much as I would have. Don't let me see you again."

After Q. left, Matt held Aaryn as she cried herself to sleep. As he did his best to console her, all he could feel was ashamed. Ashamed of what he'd almost let happen, and ashamed that, despite it all, he still wanted to get high.

But beneath it all, a small voice whispered that maybe he was ready to change.

For the third time that night he looked down at his Hammer. When was the last time he'd cleaned it? It was tarnished green from all the sweat and chemicals leaking from his pores.

Carefully, so as not to wake Aaryn, he stood up and went into the bathroom. He took off his Hammer, and using a trick he'd learned in prison, polished it with a dab of toothpaste. He admired the shine and started to put it back on. But something stopped him, that same voice in his head.

13

You don't deserve to wear the sacred Mjöllnir.
Not yet...
But one day you will.

Matt slipped his Hammer in his pocket and lay down to think about his life and what led him to this point.

The Path of Industriousness

After admitting you're an addict, the next path you must walk is the Path of Industriousness. The problem is, many Ásatrúar don't have a clear understanding of what the word industrious means. I've seen it time and again as prospective members of the Seeds of Oak Hofguild are asked to speak on each virtue. They have no problem articulating what their concept of courage or honor is, but when it comes time to explain industriousness I get a blank stare and an, "Um, it's kind of like self-reliance?"

No, *self-reliance* is kind of like self-reliance. Industriousness is something different.

Webster's Dictionary says industriousness is to be constantly, regularly, or habitually active or occupied. Synonyms are diligent or busy. It means getting off your ass and doing what needs to be done, even if you don't feel like doing it. It's rolling up your sleeves and earning your way by the sweat of your brow.

Needless to say, industriousness is a virtue that's on the decline. A healthy work ethic is being traded in for Welfare and a handout mentality. But just because a virtue isn't "popular", doesn't mean it lacks worth. The principles we live by are timeless and there will be a day when the bill for laziness and entitlement comes due. As Ásatrúar we understand that if something is worth having, it's worth working hard for.

In the Havamal, Odin often speaks about industriousness.

Stz. 37
One's own house is best,   though it is small;
        everyone is his own master at home.
He is bleeding at heart   who has to ask
        for food at every meal-tide.

Stz. 58
He should rise early   who desires to have
        another's life or property:
A sluggish wolf   seldom gets prey,
        or a sleeping man victory.

Stz. 59

He should rise early,   who has few workers,
and go and see to his work;
much remains undone   for the morning sleeper:
Wealth half depends on energy

These words show that our ancestors placed a high value on industriousness. In fact, according to Tacitus, sluggards were executed by being smothered in mud bogs. This may seem a bit extreme to our modern sensibilities, but times were harsher back then. If a farmer slacked off throughout spring and summer, then tried to leech off the community come harvest, he could cause the death of more than just himself. If a warrior tried to hide in the "shade" of the shield of the man on his right, the entire battle formation could fall into chaos. When a community is interdependent on one another, it must be understood that every man will pull his weight at the oars.

But what about those times when you're not exactly sure what your responsibility is? Should you work hard if you're not sure what you're working towards, or even if there's a smarter, more efficient way? I say that there's a fine line between industriousness and wasted effort. To illustrate my point, I'll refer to the story of Utgardaloki.

Utgardaloki

After a long journey filled with many other adventures, Thor, Loki, and their companions Thjalfi and Roskva arrived at a giant fortress. They went inside and paid their respects to the king, Utgardaloki. But while their words were polite, Utgardaloki spoke to Thor with barely concealed contempt. Not only did the king mock Thor's size, but he told the group that they could not stay in his castle if they could not show some skill or knowledge that distinguished them from everyone else.

It was well known that Thor would never shy from a challenge. But his companions were just as eager to prove themselves. Before Thor could even open his mouth, Loki addressed the king.

"Don't let my size fool you. No one in this hall has an appetite like mine. I can out-eat anyone here."

The King smiled and called forth Logi to compete against Loki. They each stood at separate ends of a table laden with all types of food. At the signal, they both began to eat until they met in the middle. Loki had devoured every crumb and picked the meat from every bone. But Logi had consumed everything in front of him, from the bones to the table itself. Therefore Logi was judged to be the winner.

Next up was Thjalfi who boasted that there wasn't a Jötun in the hall who could beat him in a race. After finding a suitable running track, Utgardaloki ordered the Jötun Hugi to race Thjalfi. After the first race it was evident that Thjalfi was no match for Hugi. Hugi had enough time to turn around and watch Thjalfi from the finish line. Thjalfi fared even worse on the second and third race, getting beaten by a bow shot. It was obvious to everyone that Thjalfi had lost.

Last up was Thor. After seeing his companions soundly beaten, he knew that it was up to him to preserve the group's reputation. He was determined to show what he was made of. So when Utgardaloki asked Thor what he wanted to compete in, Thor decided to play to his strengths.

"I challenge anyone in this hall to a drinking competition."

A drinking horn was brought out. It was longer than most horns and Thor noticed he couldn't see the end of it. He thought that was strange but put such thoughts aside as Utgardaloki explained the contest. Thor had to finish the horn in three gulps to even be considered a strong drinker.

Taking a deep breath, Thor then tipped the horn back and started to chug. When he couldn't swallow one more sip, he stopped and saw that, to his surprise, the level of the drink had barely moved! He tried two more times with nearly the same results. After the third time, the level had dropped a few inches but he had barely put a dent in the horn. Embarrassed, he had to admit defeat.

"No worries, Thor. I will try to find a competition more your speed. Do you think you can lift a little kitty cat off the ground? The children here do it all the time. Go ahead... you try."

Thor's ruddy cheeks turned crimson with anger. He knew he was being mocked. He stepped up to the cat who lay in front of the fire. Grasping it around the middle, Thor braced himself and gave a great heave...

The cat didn't budge. It gave a curious meow and the hall erupted in laughter. Furious now, Thor pulled with every fiber of muscle he had. He was rewarded with getting one paw off the ground.

"Don't hurt yourself, little fella," Utgardaloki said, wiping sweat from his brow. "It seems that cat is out of your weight class. You've failed this challenge."

"Give me one more chance."

"Are you sure? You haven't fared very well so far."

"Don't play with me, giant. One more challenge."

"Okay then. Your final challenge shall be a wrestling match."

Thor, Thurse's-Bane, slayer of Hrungnir, smiled in anticipation. This was more like it. He waited to see what giant champion the King would pit him against.

A little old giant woman hobbled into the hall. Thor paid her no mind, looking over her shoulder for his opponent.

"What are you waiting for, sonny, a written invitation?" the old woman asked, cackling with laughter.

Realizing that he was expected to fight this woman, Thor's shame knew no bounds. Still, he had agreed to the fight, and to back out now would bring further dishonor.

"I'm not going to take it easy on you, old woman," Thor said. But winning was easier said than done. Thor threw all his strength and skill into the match but the woman held her ground. Once he grew tired she brought him to one knee. Utgardaloki quickly broke them up.

The King addressed the companions, "You have failed to distinguish yourselves. You must leave this hall, but not right away. Tonight you will be my guests. Eat, drink, and get your rest. You will leave in the morning."

Thor and his companions enjoyed the King's hospitality that night and the following morning. After breakfast the King escorted them to the gate of the fortress.

"Thank you for your generosity," Thor said. "I hope you will not look down on me or the rest of the Æsir for my poor performance last night."

Utgardaloki, touched by Thor's humble tone, decided to come clean. "Listen, Asa-Thor. Now that you are on your way out of here I will tell you the truth. You and your companions did better than could be expected. In fact, there were moments when I was afraid you would accomplish the impossible. Because make no mistake, the tasks I set in front of you were impossible. I tricked you with magical illusions. The giant that Loki challenged to the eating competition was Wildfire. Thjalfi raced against Thought. When you yourself drank from the horn, the far end was submerged in the ocean. You failed to empty the horn but you lowered the sea level by inches. When you tried to lift my cat, you were really lifting the Midgard serpent. By lifting one paw up you showed your divine strength, and I was afraid you would succeed. It was an even bigger accomplishment that you stayed on your feet as long as you did when wrestling with the old woman. She is Old Age and no one wins out against her in the end."

Thor's knuckles went white as he gripped Mjöllnir. This admission did nothing to stem his anger. If anything it made it worse to know that he'd been tricked. But when he turned to vent his rage, he noticed that the King and the castle had disappeared.

Wasted Effort

In this story, Thor and his companions didn't fail due to a lack of effort. They failed due to a lack of *right* effort. They fed into the illusion of what they expected to see. By doing so, they failed to see the true nature of the challenge before them.

Imagine if Loki had researched his opponent. If he knew that he was going up against wildfire, he could've doused the table with water and easily won the competition. But if Loki, the most cunning of the Goðin, can be deceived by his own expectations, what makes us think we're any different?

But maybe the question you're asking yourself is how all of this applies to drug addiction. It's because most of us addicts think we have all the answers. This know-it-all mindset is reinforced by the fact that much of the time we *do* know more about our drug of choice than most doctors. How can someone who has never gotten high tell us about the effects of a drug, or how it feels to withdraw? We know everything there is to know about using.

The problem is that now we're facing something we know nothing about: Permanent recovery. This is uncharted territory. I'll be the first to admit that when I started this book I had a thorough misconception of what addiction is. I viewed addiction as a personality flaw. I saw addicts as weak people who just lacked the willpower to quit. If I could just find the right words to say, I could convince my brothers to stop getting high. But time after time I was let down. Frustrated. But like Thor wrestling with old age, it was all because I didn't understand my opponent.

That's why on the Path of Industriousness you will take the time to learn everything you can about addiction and recovery.

An in-depth analysis of every drug is beyond the scope of this book. Much has been written on this subject, and for those who have access to the internet, there's a wealth of information, some good, some not so good. For our purposes here, a short summary of the major hard drugs will have to suffice.

Opiates

The earliest mention of the poppy plant was around 3500 BC, but it wasn't until the 11th century AD that it was introduced to Europe by an Arab scholar, Avicenna. Since then its popularity has grown with every passing century.

Opium is extracted from the sap of *Papaver somniferum.* It contains alkaloids such as morphine, codeine, narcotine, narceine, and thebaine, among others. Through the purification process, the percentage of morphine increases. (An interesting note, the word morphine is derived from Morpheus, the Greek god of dreams.)

In 1898, after searching for the perfect opiate, one that relieved pain and wasn't addictive, Heinrich Dreser created heroin. He was at least half right. After heroin was found to be extremely addictive it went underground, which is where we are today.

With heroin, the user becomes invincible and guarded against everyday cares, fears, and pain. It is a paradox of warmth and icy coolness, as if the head is cut off from the rest of the body. Many addicts describe a sense of isolation, calculation, and perfect memory. But the removal of all fear is perhaps the greatest draw in this day and age.

But the cost is great. There are no shortcuts to the spiritual bliss that opium gives a glimpse of. The physical and psychological condition of the addict eventually deteriorates.

And withdrawal is its own type of hell. According to Van Epen, the symptoms of opiate withdrawal are: A fearful, restless and rather caved in countenance, cold and clammy skin, large eyes with dilated pupils, a runny nose, hiccups, constant yawning, a feeling of being alternately hot and cold, stomach cramps with a great deal of flatulence and diarrhea, sometimes vomiting, muscular pains and cramps in the back of the legs, hair standing on end, increased intestinal movement, slightly raised pulse rate, blood pressure, and body temperature, and an unquenchable desire to take more opiates.

The worst symptoms can last for a few days and nights. But even once the worst is over, the addict is irritable, sensitive, easily tired but unable to sleep, and depressed. This can last for several months but the environmental factors play a role. Needless to say, withdrawing in a prison cell is less ideal than withdrawing in a comfortable room. Being around negative and fearful people can increase the level of anxiety the addict faces.

Cocaine

It may be interesting to know that cocaine, once considered the "rich man's drug" was first introduced by a bunch of poor farmers. During an expedition to South America in the 16th century, Amerigo Vespucci wrote: "They were very ugly in appearance and in their habits. They all puffed up their cheeks with a green herb on which they chewed constantly like cows. They could hardly speak and they all wore two gourds around their neck. One was full of the herb which everyone had in their mouth, the other was full of a white flour which looked like plaster. From time to time they would moisten a stick, put it in the flour and place it in their mouths... In this way they mixed the flour with the herb... and because we were very surprised by this we could not understand their secret."

The natives chewed these coca leaves for endurance and used them in religious rituals. The leaves would eventually be exported to Europe and used in wines, champagnes, cigarettes, and even soft drinks like Coca-Cola. It was used in many different ways, such as: a means to kick morphine and alcohol addiction, a cold and flu remedy, an anaesthetic for dentists and eye surgeons, and as a performance enhancer for soldiers. The first mention of it being snorted was in 1900 in The Journal of American Medical Association. "The Negroes in some parts of the South are reported as being addicted to a new form of vice, that of cocaine 'snuffing' or the 'coke habit'!"

The effects of cocaine are threefold: anaesthetic, stimulant, and euphoric. It blocks the conduct of stimuli by the sensory nerves, increases respiration, heartbeat, and blood pressure. It also greatly increases energy and stamina. The user feels smarter, more confident, and has an increased libido. That's why it is so popular as a party drug because it helps people overcome any insecurities or inhibitions. The effects of this false sense of security, however, are cynicism and a lack of empathy or sensitivity.

Even though cocaine isn't physically addictive, the psychological withdrawal can be intense. There can be paranoid fears and tactile hallucinations such as "coke bugs". The user can feel like he's being persecuted or watched by cops. In order to suppress these symptoms, many coke addicts turn to alcohol, sleeping pills, tranquillizers or heroin. According to Van Epen, for weeks or months "The cocaine depression can resemble a vital endogenous depression accompanied by a sombre fearful mood, the lack of perspective on life, complete indifference and apathy. The victims are extremely tired and lacking in energy. They do not sleep, they do not eat, they cannot cry and are often suicidal."

The long-term effects of chronic cocaine use are an increase rate of heart attack, stroke, and kidney failure. The nostrils can blister and perforate. Extreme weight loss and the atrophying of muscles is common. Also there is an increased chance of miscarriage and birth defects with women who use cocaine while pregnant.

Amphetamines

Amphetamine was first synthesized in the late 1800s, but methamphetamine wasn't discovered until 1919. It was used to cure narcolepsy and as a weight loss remedy. Hyperactive children were given small doses to calm them down. During the Second World War it was given to soldiers to fight exhaustion and to encourage reckless, agressive behavior.

In the late 60s, early 70s, speed got a deservedly bad reputation. The speed freak was a dangerous phenomenon in the hippie era because of his impulsive and violent behavior. In places like Haight Ashbury, concerned hippies put up posters saying "Speed Kills" and "Meth is Death." Eventually because of this violence and increased legal regulation, the interest in meth fell off.

The effects of amphetamines are similar to cocaine. The user feels energetic, confident, and more intelligent. Ideas pop up with an increased rapidity. The user often becomes more aggressive and sexually active than usual.

Using amphetamines is like burning a candle at both ends. We don't know exactly how sleep rejuvenates our physical body, but we can see what the lack of sleep does to the addict. There are sores which do not heal, brittle fingernails and tooth decay known as "meth mouth". The heart and lungs see all sorts of complications and neuroses often develop. Overall, the body begins to break down. Like cocaine, meth is not physically addictive but the psychological effect is insidious. The user feels that the next hit will make him feel better, when it's really prolonging his destruction.

The worst parts of withdrawal are over in a matter of days, but the long term psychological effects can last a lifetime.

Matt's Saga

Later that same night, Matt lay in bed with Aaryn beside him. She kept tossing and turning in her sleep. He tried to soothe her by stroking her hair the way she liked, but nothing seemed to work.

Unable to sleep himself, he finally pulled out his phone. Up until now he'd used his phone for exactly two reasons: To call his dealer and to watch porn. Right now he wasn't in the mood for either.

He searched for Rehab spots and spent a while researching his options. There weren't a whole lot. Sure, there were some nice places, ones with tennis courts, sandy beaches, and spas, but they were way too expensive.

He needed to find a way to get clean on his own, for free, without his PO finding out. So he started researching what he could on the effects of cocaine and Xanax and how to detox safely.

Some of the stuff he learned was encouraging. For example, cocaine wasn't physically addictive which meant the only withdrawal symptoms would be psychological. If he could get past the cravings he would be okay. Xanax, on the other hand, was physically addictive. There were cases of people having seizures and dying from withdrawal; however, Matt wasn't too worried. He only used Xanax once or twice a week when he was having trouble sleeping.

Matt also learned something else interesting. He had planned to buy a bunch of beer in the hopes that getting drunk would make withdrawing easier. But apparently, people who abuse alcohol and cocaine together create a new enzyme in their bodies that make each substance more addictive than when used alone. Basically, getting drunk would fan the flames of his crack addiction.

By the time he put the phone down, the battery was almost dead and Sunna's first rays peeked through the window. Although he was tired, he had learned a lot, filling nearly five pages of a yellow pad with notes.

The hard part was still to come, but at least now he had an idea of what he was facing. He kissed the back of Aaryn's neck and went to sleep.

The Path Of Courage

On the Path of Courage we take our newly acquired knowledge of self and addiction and make a decision to stop using. Or, as the Odinist AA group in Ramsey Unit, Texas so aptly put it. "We make a decision to align ourselves with the Goðin and to contribute constructively to the Tapestry of Wyrd."

You may ask why the first two paths were necessary. If it's just a matter of making the decision to change, what was the point of all that introspection and research? It's because courage without knowledge is recklessness. In war we fight to win, not for a glorious defeat.

Herman the Cheruscan, a great hero of our Folk, comes to mind. Every year on the ninth of Shedding (September) we celebrate his victory over the Roman Legions. That a German tribesman defeated one of the greatest military powers is a testament to his genius. Looking at it from the hindsight of history, his victory at Teutoberger Wald can be broken into three separate causes:

1. Self-Knowledge or truth. Hermann assessed the strengths and weaknesses of his fellow tribesman.
2. Industriousness. While serving as a Roman soldier he also analyzed his enemy. He knew their battle tactics and how they would respond in a given situation. Also while acting as an emissary to the tribes he was able to study the terrain and weed out informants.
3. Courage. All the knowledge in the world is useless without right action. When the time came to act, Hermann did not hesitate. He fought a guerilla war that pushed the Romans out of Germania.

Hermann's motivation was clear: To stave off the destruction of his culture, his people, and his homeland.

You're armed with almost everything you need to act. All that's left is to uncover *your* motivation.

What's Your "Why"?

As a goði, I've had many brothers tell me they want to get off hard drugs when really all they want is for me to get off their ass. They think it's what I want to hear and will say whatever they have to in order to keep my respect while continuing to use drugs.

Some guys will see the example that other clean-living members set and will want their approval. These guys are often huge disappointments. They clean up and toe the line... for a while. Then once they get comfortable in the community, or start hanging with other addicts, they revert back to old ways.

The truth is, the next man's hamingja and willpower can only carry you so far. So while it's important to surround yourself with men and women you respect and admire, when it comes to addiction, it's more important to want to change at your core.

Up until this point you've only admitted that you are an addict, not that you want to change. Now would be a good time to ask yourself an important question: Do you really want to quit using drugs? There's no wrong answer. A negative answer can save you a lot of pointless reading. It can also stop you from reinforcing the habit of failure. Make no mistake, failure can become a habit which weakens your resolve, which leads to more failure, which... well, you get the picture. Its like the Midgard Serpent biting its own tail; a vicious circle of poison.

As Ásatrúar we don't **try**, we **do**. We are not our thoughts, wishes, fantasies, or hopes; we are our **actions**. So unless you have a burning desire to change, a needfire that will carry you through the bleakest night, then don't waste your time. Come back when you've hit rock bottom.

Are you still here? Great. Now let's talk about motivation. There are two types, extrinsic and intrinsic.

An extrinsic motivation is any motivation that is formed by someone else's values. It's founded on something outside of yourself. Extrinsic motivations are rarely effective when it comes to lasting change. "I want to kick drugs so I can hang out with the Hammer guys. They seem to have their shit together." Fail. What happens when they're not around? Can you stand on your own? Or... "My girlfriend won't have sex with me when I'm high, so I'll quit for her."

Another fail. When push comes to shove it's probably easier just to find a new girlfriend.

It's commendable to want to be a better person for those you care about. However, the approval of your family, friends, and fellow heathens is little consolation when you're kicking dope and you hurt so bad you'd blow your head off if a gun was handy. Times like that you've gotta want it real bad for yourself.

Since an addict's success or failure comes down to the power of his motivation, it would make sense to find one that will carry you to victory. That's where intrinsic motivations come in.

An intrinsic motivation arises from your deepest convictions and personal values. They're what you would believe if everything was stripped from you. Every one of our Goðin work from intrinsic motivations.

Odin: To grow wiser by any means in order to stave off Ragnarok as long as possible.

Thor: To achieve self-mastery through direct action in order to protect Midgard from the forces of chaos.

Now take some time to figure out your why. What motivates you to want to change? Once again, there's no wrong answer as long as it's **your** truth. When you're finished, write it down. Return to it often for courage, especially when times get hard.

What Are You So Afraid Of?

Everyone knows the feeling: Life is running smoothly, lookin' good, feelin' good, when suddenly something comes along to throw a wrench in your day. Maybe the doctor hesitates a moment too long when reading your chart; maybe you're asked to give a presentation in front of a group of people; or maybe someone simply cuts you in line. Almost instantaneously your hands get clammy, your heart beats faster, and your mouth either dries up or secretes *way* too much saliva.

This process is called arousal and it's not the fun kind. When these physiological stressors occur, it doesn't mean you're a coward, it means you're the result of hundreds of thousands of years of evolution. Our brains process information via the amygdala, located in the temporal lobes. The amygdala is like the Heimdall of our brain, constantly on alert, scanning for threats. This served us well when our environment was filled with actual threats, such as roving wolf packs and warring tribes. Problem is, it's not effective at differentiating real threats from threats to our ego or even figments of our imagination. It automatically sends us into fight, flight, or freeze mode, activating the hypothalamic, pituitary, and adrenal glands. These in turn pump you full of adrenaline and cortisol, which, depending on the situation, have you ready to snap, or trembling like a little girl.

According to the lore, Hoenir gifted us with memory, fancy (imagination), and will. These traits are a blessing in that they separate us from animals who act from pure instinct. But they can also be a curse. Memories of bad experiences in the past are often projected into the future, causing dread and anxiety. Our imaginations can conjure up an infinite number of misfortunes which may never come. All they do is expend energy as we get stuck in a loop of chronic worrying.

Odin warns us about this in the Havamal, st. 23.

Stz. 23
A foolish man   is awake all night,
        pondering everything;
    he is tired   when morning breaks
        and nothing has changed.

Think about it: How many times have you needlessly worried about something that hasn't happened yet? It happens to me all the time. I'll have an issue with someone and won't be able to straighten it right away. I'll build the confrontation up in my head where it starts out as an argument and ends with us stabbing each other up. But experience has taught me three things:
1. Things you imagine rarely happen.
2. When they do happen, they're rarely as bad as you imagined.
3. If bad things are going to happen, worrying about them beforehand only prolongs your suffering.

But what does this have to do with drug addiction? It's simple; you show me someone who's addicted to drugs, and I'll show you someone who's afraid of something.

David Hawkins, MD, PhD, has this to say: "The clinical degrees of fearfulness are expressed as anxiety disorders, including phobias, PTSD, inhibitions, or excesses of compensatory mechanisms such as withdrawal, dependency, or substance addiction. Widespread use of tranquilizers and alcohol attests to the problem of uncomfortable and excessive anxiety."

What this means to those of us without doctorates is that people use drugs as a bandaid to cover up fear. If we are to quit using drugs, at some point we will have to deal with our fear. That is what the Path of Courage is all about.

Cultivating Courage

One day on the Yard I was talking to my buddy Jughead about courage. I'd just had to kick a guy out of the Hofguild for cowardice and made the comment that "you can't teach heart." Basically, that courage is either in you or it isn't. Jughead disagreed and asked me if I was scared of the dark as a kid. I told him I was. "What did your parents do? They gave you a nightlight and then eventually took that away, too. Are you still scared of the dark?"

Needless to say it made me rethink what I thought was a catchy saying. I can admit when I'm wrong, especially since the idea that I can help instill courage in people is better than the alternative.

Let me be upfront; even though courage is the third step in this program, I believe it is the most important virtue for a new Ásatrúar to focus on. And I'm not talking about the chest-thumping, rumble anyone who disrespects you, type of courage. (Although, that too has its place.) I'm talking about the courage to stand up for your beliefs and also to face your own shortcomings.

So if our personal evolution and our drug recovery depend on cultivating courage, what are we waiting for? Let's talk about how we can do so. Here are a few tactics you can use.

1. **Box Breathing:** I learned this technique from Mark Divine who learned it from the SEALS. It's breathing with a 4:4:4:4 rhythm. Four second inhale, hold for four seconds; Four second exhale, hold for four seconds. Repeat. What this does is "reset" your nervous system from all those fear systems. The idea is that, by controlling the symptoms of fear, you control the fear

itself. Matter over mind. Believe it or not, it works.

2. **Meditations:** Find a quiet time when you won't be disturbed. Regulate your breathing and choose one of the following to contemplate:
    - What does living a courageous life look like?
    - If the Norns have already decided the day of your death, and you truly believe this, what is there to be afraid of?
    - Think of the courage and heroism of your ancestors and how the same blood runs through your veins.
    - What does the saying "Do good and fear nothing" mean?

3. **The joy of living dangerously:** This technique requires some balls. Take stock of the things that scare you and face them, one by one. Really lean into your fears. I recently did this when it came to my phobia of doctors and disease. After years of fucking whores and getting prison tattoos I was justifiably/irrationaly terrified of having a blood test done. I spent years worrying about HIV and Hep C. It was so bad that when I finally did decide to get tested I had to get my cellie to turn in the medical slip. But now that I know I'm clean, it's like a weight has been lifted. It's like that with any fear you overcome. Energy that was wasted propping up that fear is now available for other, more useful purposes. And you'll find out that once you face a few of your fears, it quickly gets easier.

4. **"What then?"** The purpose of this game is to get to the origin of your fears. The technique comes from Hawkins' Transcending Levels of Consciousness but it's something we all naturally do when we get stuck in fear loops. The only difference is we don't follow the chain of fear to its logical and cathartic conclusion. Start with a specific fear and then surrender the consequence if it should come true. Here's an example:
I'm afraid I'll lose my job.
And then what?
And then I won't have any money.
And then what?
And then I won't be able to get high.
And then what?
And then my friends and my girl will leave.

And then what?

And then I will be alone with my thoughts.

And then what?

And then I'll have to relive my experiences in the war (childhood abuse, death of a loved one, etc.).

And then what?

And I might not be strong enough and want to kill myself.

It's easy to see that most of our fears end with a fear of death. If we can overcome this fear by surrendering to it, we can overcome anything.

Making Your Oath

Up until now, every step you have taken has been in the realm of thought. You have admitted you are an addict, researched your addiction, and analyzed your fears. This is a necessary foundation, but by itself it's not enough.

It's time to take action.

Armed with a greater knowledge of yourself, now you can fight the Jötnar of drug addiction and hope to win. You can expect to be the victor in your battle for sobriety, instead of just another casualty of war.

But like any warrior getting ready to go into battle, you first must declare your intention with an oath. This oath isn't to any particular person or country; however, it's an oath that from this day forward you will quit using hard drugs.

Before going any further, I want to clarify just how important oaths are in this way of life. A man's honor rests upon his word and the worst punishments in the afterlife are reserved for oath breakers and murderers. Every word that comes out of your mouth is either an oath, a troth, or a promise, but words spoken to the Goðin are especially binding. These oaths are not only binding to you, but also any of your fellow Ásatrúar who witness and accept the oath. Breaking an oath diminishes the hamingja (luck, personal power) of everyone involved.

Because of this, many Ásatrúar may be hesitant to accept the oath of an addict. Don't take this personally, or as a sign that they want to see you fail. In the Seeds of Oak, there are a number of ways that we deal with the complexities of oaths. The first is that we don't give or take lightly. Generally, the only time we make group oaths are during the High Holy Days. The second is that the goði designates an oath caller, usually an elder in the community. A week before the formal oaths are made, the oath caller will listen to each person's oath and deem whether or not it is achievable. If the oath caller believes the oath can't be accepted, they will help the member reword it or come up with one that will be. And lastly, difficult oaths are paired with wergild in case the member falls short. This shouldn't be viewed as a cop out, and the wergild should be something with a bite to it.

That being said, it's not necessary for the oath you're about to make to be witnessed by a group of people. This can be between you and the Goðin. Right now, make an oath to complete the rest of this program, and to stop doing drugs for nine weeks. Nine is a holy number and it will imbue your effort with divine purpose. Make this oath aloud. Just speak from your heart and know that the Goðin are listening.

Matt's Saga

The next morning Matt woke to find Aaryn carpet surfing for stray crack rocks. The sight of it broke his heart and reinforced his urge to get clean. He called for her to come back to bed.

"Just a second. I think we dropped some when we were partying the other night."

Matt sighed. He couldn't judge her. He'd done worse, much worse, to get high. After last night he'd faced some hard truths. He was poison to her, had been since the night they'd met at an ODU party and he'd offered her an X pill. It was the first time she'd ever gotten high.

His own addictions went back much further. He couldn't remember a time when he wasn't stealing forties from Food Lion or selling blunts to kids in school. Once his dad left, his house became the party spot. It was cool back then, but Matt realized that's when his problems had really started.

Another hard truth: He had never really conquered his addictions in prison. Sure, he rarely got high. But that was just because drugs rarely hit the Yard, and when they did, they were too expensive. Not to mention, his Ásatrú brothers looked down on people who got strung out. So he toed the line and snorted strip on the low every once in a while.

"C'mon Aaryn, let's just lay in bed today."

"Kay. I'll call Eternity and get us some Xannys."

"Why don't we chill, you know, clean up."

There was a long pause as Aaryn tried to judge whether he was playing. Then she snapped. "You're joking right? I was clean for five years while you were locked up doing god knows what. Now when it's time for me to have a little fun, you're on some holier than thou kick?"

"It's not like that."

"Then pop a Bar, mellow out, and we'll figure out a way to get right."

"No. I'm good."

"Yeah, whatever. Call me when you're done being a pussy."

Aaryn stormed out of the room and Matt was too exhausted to chase after her. The little voice told him this was for the best. There was no way he could handle his and her recovery.

Matt rubbed the Hammer in his pocket. Closing his eyes, he silently made an oath to the Goðin and his ancestors to get clean.

He staggered to the door and closed it. The room was paid up through next week. Thinking that far ahead scared him shitless. He would have to summon all his courage. The next few days were gonna suck.

The Path Of Discipline

Discipline is key to successful recovery. No matter how much truth and courage you've shown up to this point, if you don't have the discipline necessary to order your life in a way that is conducive to staying clean, you will hit a dead end.

For many people, the word discipline conjures up images of repression and abuse. They're confusing punishment with discipline. But as I'll show you, discipline, when used correctly, can make you more free and powerful, not less.

Odin is a prime example of power through discipline. The Allfather lives on mead alone; he feeds all solid food to his wolves Geri and Freki. Now, before we take this to mean that Odin is a wino, let's break it down symbolically.

When you come across the word "mead" in the lore, take a close look at who's drinking it. When it's a Saga dealing with humans, mead is usually just mead. But when it involves the Goðin or other supernatural beings, mead has a higher meaning. It represents wisdom, higher consciousness, poetry or wit. Odin is willing to sacrifice all in the pursuit of these ideals. He hung from the World Tree nine nights for a single sip from Mímirsbrunnr and seduced Gunnlod to steal the Byrgir mead.

Just imagine tasting the sweet mead of wisdom as Odin has. All other knowledge and experience would be bland by comparison. Inferior. As he feasts in Valhalla, Odin feeds all solid food to Geri and Freki, *Greed* and "Gluttony." The pork they eat is delicious, the same food that the Einherjar feast on. But Odin has chosen to sublimate his base desires for higher virtues.

How many of you could trade the pork chop in front of you for the smallest chance of gaining true wisdom? Nietzsche said it best; "The mark of the higher man is the ability for delayed gratification.". As Ásatrúar and Odinists we should constantly strive to transcend our limitations. In order to break the chains of thralldom and sip from the well of wisdom, we have to set aside the drugs that are holding us down.

Praying won't work. Wishing won't work. A tru man takes responsibility for his right to be free.

Detoxing

You've made the decision to stop using and have armed yourself with relevant information about your drug of choice. Now here comes the hard part, the part that everyone dreads; the crash. The next few days will require a strong will and valiant heart. When times get tough, remember our Folk heroes who endured unimaginable pain. Guthroth's tongue was cut out. Raud the Strong was forced to swallow a snake. Eyvind Kinnrifi had a bowl of hot embers placed on his stomach until it burst. I'm sure you can endure some cramps and nausea.

Before going any further, however, I need to make something clear. So far I've used the word drugs as a blanket term for all addictive substances. But we all know that every drug is different, from the way it affects the brain, to the protocol for detoxing. Some drugs like methamphetamine and cocaine are not dangerous to withdraw from physiologically. Other drugs such as opiates, certain benzodiazepines like Xanax, and alcohol can leave you toes up. Withdrawal from these drugs can cause tremors, seizures, hallucinations, or death.

I would seriously recommend that you consult with a physician when attempting to detox. Withdrawal can be debilitating and may stir up repressed emotions. Severe cases of depression can even lead to suicide. A physician will be aware of these risks and can take measures to ease the pain and alleviate mental distress.

Another reason to work with a physician is it stops you from self-medicating. Let's face it, self-medicating is what got you into this mess. This is the one time during this program where its okay to give up control. Until this poison is flushed from your system, your mind can be your worst enemy. So find a physician you trust and hand the reins over.

Your physician will probably start you off on a short term prescription to get you through the worst part. Urine screening may be mandatory. Keep in mind that doctors, especially those who specialize in addiction, are used to seeing the worst in people. Just be patient and follow instructions. Once he sees you're sincere about recovery, he will be more encouraged to help.

Identifying Triggers

During and after detox, it's important to assess your triggers. A trigger is anything that has the potential to derail your recovery and cause you to relapse. Sometimes a trigger is obvious and can be managed with a little forethought. But often a trigger is subtle and by the time you realize you're in the grip of one, it takes a supreme act of will to overcome.

In order to work this step you will need to identify your triggers and develop strategies to avoid or work around them.

I'll give a personal example. One of my triggers is dealing drugs. I learned this about myself after catching a distribution charge when I was 19. While on pretrial release I had to lay low. The cops raided my house and were pulling me over every time I stepped out the door. Knowing they only had to get lucky once, I quit dealing until everything died down. My drug use up until this point had started to get out of control. I was cutting out a bag for personal use. Hell, it was all profit, I told myself. I wasn't like my customers who were paying **real** money. They were the junkies despite the fact that they might be doing just a gram on the weekends and I was up to an eightball a night. Rationalization at its finest.

But the strange thing was, when I stopped dealing, the urge to get high went away. In fact, it was much harder for me to quit dealing drugs than it was to quit doing them.

Now we'll identify other common triggers and strategies to manage them.

- **Boredom:** This is a big one, especially in prison where one day seems to bleed into the next. Drugs make you feel good (at least temporarily) and allow you to forget how boring your life is (for a short time). But when they wear off, you have no choice but to face reality. Wouldn't it be better to not live a mundane life? As cliché as it may sound, this is the only life you have. Find your purpose and live it.
- **Places from your past:** Maybe it's a house which brings up painful memories. Or, on the other hand, it could be somewhere that reminds you of an exciting time in your life. Pain and nostalgia can both fuel drug abuse, as you subconsciously associate certain places with it. For serious issues, you may

37

need to seek therapy to address the underlying issue. Otherwise, you should remind yourself that you're no longer the same person you were back then or avoid the place altogether.

- **Certain People:** We all have that one friend who brings out the worst in us. Often you love hanging out with them because they're the life of the party, but you always seem to regret it afterwards. When you're getting sober, you have to avoid other addicts like the plague. If you can let them know with a straightforward conversation, great. But often they will see this as a threat to your "friendship" (or their ego) and will do whatever they can to pull you into their negativity. It may be better to view them as enemies to your sobriety and use cunning to avoid them

- **Stress:** Problems with money, work, or relationships can lead to stress which in turn leads to getting high. It's easier to load a shot and drift away than to deal with responsibilities. But when the high has faded and the drugs are gone, the responsibilities and stress are still there, waiting. Only now you're just a little more broke and defeated. The best way to deal with this trigger is to learn more effective stress management techniques.

- **Creative Blocks:** This trigger is a big one for creative types such as artists and writers. There's a prevalent stereotype of the tortured artist using drugs to fuel creativity. It's bullshit. I've written books sober and high out of my mind and the ones I wrote high sucked. Ideas that seemed good when I was under the influence were fucking stupid when I sobered up. Most artists *feel* more creative because the drugs lower inhibitions and silence the inner critic. Still, there are better, less damaging ways to do this.

- **And when things are just going *too* good:** This trigger might be hard to believe. When life is going smoothly, why would someone want to throw a stick in the spokes? But I see it all the time, the self-destructive tendencies of people who just don't think they deserve to be happy. If you feel you may suffer from this insidious trigger, you need to get *more* disciplined the better things get, not less. Resist the urge to loosen up by reminding yourself that discipline is what got you this far in the first place.

This is by no means a complete list of all triggers. It's just meant to give you an idea of the possibilities. The important thing is to examine your own patterns and come up with strategies and habits to address them.

Healthy Habits

After the worst of your withdrawal is over, it's time to institute positive habits in your life. Laying in your bed, eating Cheetos and watching Law and Order reruns isn't going to cut it. At this point you're probably feeling a great deal of anxiety. That's understandable, considering the huge upheaval you've created in your life. But in order to offset this anxiety and ensure that stress doesn't chip away at your willpower, it's important that you focus on the Big Three.

Sleep. Nutrition. Exercise. This may seem basic, but good advice usually is. These three factors are foundational to your physical health and emotional resiliency.

We'll start with sleep. Too little of it causes you to be short tempered and moody. No shit, right? But did you know it's because the brain reverts to a more primitive state? The amygdala goes into high gear, throwing logic out the window and making you simultaneously more emotional, and less able to deal with emotions. Getting a good night's sleep can work miracles. The problem is, getting to sleep can *take* a miracle. Every recovering addict knows the frustrating feeling. You're dragging ass all day, just waiting for the moment when you can fall into bed, but when you finally do, suddenly you're wide awake. Some tips to fight insomnia: Keep your room as dark as possible with no distractions. Don't drink caffeine within hours of going to bed, and drink milk if it helps. At this point in your recovery, don't focus so much on regulating your sleep time, just focus on getting enough. At least eight hours, preferably with uninterrupted REM sleep.

Next up is nutrition. I can't stress how important this is. Your body is trying to recover from years of abuse and neglect. Its healing capabilities are remarkable, but you need to do your part. Your body and brain will welcome a diet that includes plenty of nutrient-rich fruits and vegetables, some complete proteins, and healthy fatty acids such as olive oil. When it comes to carbs, whole grain complex carbs give you the most bang for your brain. And it should go without saying that the food you put in your body should be the cleanest you can afford. Haven't you put enough unpronounceable chemicals in your body for one lifetime?

The last of the Big 3 is exercise. The effects of exercise can dramatically change your life. Not only does getting ripped help physically, it also helps mentally, brotein shake. Exercise regulates the release of dopamine, seratonin, and noradrenaline. Since drug abuse throws these chemicals out of whack, regulation is just what you need. As an added benefit, exercise flushes the stress hormone cortisol out of your system. So if you can push past the initial reluctance of working out, you'll end up feeling better than when you started.

Sleep. Nutrition. Exercise. It's easy to see how these three things build on each other. With adequate sleep you have the willpower to resist unhealthy foods and the energy to exercise. With proper nutrition you have restful sleep and fuel for your workouts. And with exercise you maintain high metabolism and burn off excess stress and energy which helps you sleep. Conversely, an imbalance in one of these can negatively impact the other two. It's up to you to find wunjo, or harmony, in your lifestyle habits.

Changing Habits

But what if the inertia to develop new, healthy habits seems impossible to overcome? It can be disheartening. Our sagas are filled with strong-willed men who accomplished legendary feats, and yet we struggle to stick to a workout plan, or go to bed at a reasonable time. If you set out to change your habits with the best of intentions, only to slack up and fail, don't feel bad. (Don't get complacent and quit either.) A big reason why you fail is lack of understanding and improper technique.

So what exactly *is* a habit? A habit is a shortcut or ritual that allows your brain to operate on autopilot, conserving energy for conscious thought and decision-making. In fact, that's what we'll call habits from now on, rituals, to break you of the habit of thinking of them in a positive or negative light.

Think of the rituals you act out every day. Tying your shoes, brushing your teeth. If you're in prison you stand for count. If you're in the military you perform drills. After enough repetition, these rituals become so ingrained that you do them without thinking. In fact, with rituals like the military drill, you perform it *so* you can do it without thinking.

These rituals are a benefit to your brain. If you had to consciously think about every inconsequential thing you did, your brain would tire more quickly. Every conscious thought or action draws a little energy from the brain's "gas tank." This is why it's nearly impossible to change a bad ritual, or enact a good ritual, using willpower alone. At the first opportunity, the brain will go with the ritual it is most comfortable with, the ritual that takes less energy.

So if your brain is your own worst enemy, how do you work against it? The answer is, you have to use cunning. Establishing positive rituals or eliminating bad ones involves the same basic skills: Intention and follow through.

With intention, the first step is to pinpoint your goal. In order for a goal to be successful, it should have a few key components. It should be charged with emotion. A goal you're not passionate about is almost certain to fail. Also, ideally, each goal should follow the SMART system. (SMART is an acronym for Specific, Measurable, Attainable, Realistic, and Timed). Once you have clarified your goal using SMART, the next step is to write it down. Lastly you should visualize yourself going through the necessary steps to achieve the goal.

Follow through is where your cunning comes in. Remember the amygdala and its fight, flight, or freeze reactions? Well, these also come into play with rituals. If you try to implement a change that is too far from the status quo, it shocks the system and you freeze or fail. That's why most New Year's resolutions are a bust. People try to do a complete 180 overnight and their brain revolts, self-sabotaging their well intended plans.

But there is a solution and it's called kaizen. And while it may sound Japanese, it was first developed by the U. S. military. (It's also the only reason this book was actually completed.) The nuts and bolts of kaizen is making small decisions and actions, or "continuous improvement", instead of big ones.

Here's an example. Say your Yule resolution is to start running every morning. But after the first morning you realize January is fucking cold and your enthusiasm starts to wane. Using kaizen you would break the run into micro goals. First you would resolve to wake up on time. Next you would resolve to eat a run-worthy breakfast. Further goals might be to get dressed in your running gear, stretch, and walk outside. After each goal is completed you give yourself permission to quit, but once you set a micro goal it has to be done. What usually happens, however, is the first few victories will snowball until you're outside pounding the pavement. Eventually the entire process will become its own ritual and you will no longer need to set micro goals.

The reason kaizen works is because the actions you're completing are so small and incremental, they operate below the threshold of the amygdala's threat analysis system.

Kaizen can be used to stick to healthy habits or avoid triggers. But it can also be used to stay sober. When the urge to get high takes over, don't think about having to stay sober for the rest of your life. That can overwhelm you. Instead, break your sobriety down into whatever increment you can handle. A week. A day. Five minutes.

Summing it all up

A lot has been asked of you on the Path of Discipline. You've identified the triggers that cause you to relapse and countered them with coping strategies. You've regulated your emotions with proper sleep, nutrition, and exercise. And you've learned methods to create positive rituals along with ways of making sure you stick to them. With your newfound discipline and confidence you're now ready for the next Path.

Matt's Saga

Matt wouldn't have wished the past three days on his worst enemy.

It had started out okay. Exhausted, he'd sunk into a deep sleep for sixteen hours. But after that, sleep was impossible. Every muscle in his body ached and his head felt like someone shoved an icepick through the temple. Stomach cramps had him curled up in the fetal position. The Oxys and Xannys he'd been popping "just to sleep" had stopped by to say hi.

To make matters worse, he had a dim memory of Aaryn coming over. She'd been concerned and offered him a pill to feel better. He called her a junkie bitch. A lamp might've been thrown.

Now he peeked over the edge of his pillow. Shards of glass littered the floor. Yeah, a lamp had been thrown.

At least the worst seemed to be over. He staggered into the shower and let the hot water scald away the sweat and grime. Then he drank as much water as his stomach could stand, got dressed, and headed out, slipping a "Do Not Disturb" sign on the door. He pitied the maid who would have to clean that room.

He didn't stay gone long. Just long enough to cash his check and buy groceries. Back at the motel he complained about the water pressure and asked to switch rooms. The old room had too many drug memories, not to mention Aaryn still had a key.

He moved into the new room. Over the next few days he settled into a strict routine, reminiscent of prison. In the mornings he would do sit-ups and pushups, take a shower, and fix a healthy breakfast. He only took on afternoon shifts at the bar he worked at and would leave the second his shift was over. The nights were the worst. That's when the temptation to get high was the strongest. The first night, his hands shaking, he'd erased every number from his phone even remotely tied to the drug game. Now he spent most nights watching nature documentaries or reading his Ásatrú Edda.

It wasn't the most exciting life but these small rituals brought him comfort and a sense of discipline. He'd even considered setting up a small altar and maybe, just maybe, calling his P. O....

The Path of Hospitality

"All that which you do will return to you, sooner or later, for good or for ill. Thus strive always to do good to others, or at least strive always to be just."

Norse Rede of Honor

It cannot be overstated how important hospitality was to our ancestors. When you lived in a harsh environment where food was scarce and vast distances separated one settlement from another, an inhospitable person could literally be the death of another. There were strict rules governing one's conduct toward the traveler. Barring that they were not outlaws you were required to give them food, water, and shelter for a minimum of three nights. To deny them this was dishonorable, not to mention dangerous. One never knew if the traveler being turned away was Odin, the Wanderer.

Odin had a lot to say on hospitality. The Havamal is filled with wise advice on how to treat those around you. Every time I reread it, I'm amazed at how down to earth and practical the wisdom is. This is no pie-in-the-sky, utopian view of how the world works. No "turn the other cheek" and everyone's your brother bullshit. It is realistic and timeless advice that can be followed successfully in any situation.

The virtue of hospitality can be summed up in five stanzas from the Havamal.

True friends are important... "Know if you have a friend whom you fully trust, and would get good from him, you should blend your mind with his and exchange gifts, and go to see him often." Hav. 44.

You should look out for them... "To his friend a man should be a friend, and requite gifts with gifts; men should receive laughter with laughter, but leasing with lying." Hav. 42

It doesn't always have to be much... "Something great is not always to be given, often little will purchase praise; with half a loaf and a half-drained cup I got myself a comrade." Hav. 52.

And don't overstay your welcome... "A guest should depart, not always stay in one place. The welcome becomes unwelcome if he continues too long in another's house." Hav. 35.

But to your enemy you owe nothing... "If there is another whom you trust little, yet would get good from him, you should speak fairly of him, but think falsely, and pay a lie for a lie." Hav. 45.

This advice is common sense. Be good to your friends and family. Don't be a burden. Don't support your enemy. But all too often it seems that common sense is the least common thing of all.

I'd be willing to bet that, throughout your addiction, your actions have run counter to the advice above. As addicts, we have a front-sight focus on getting high, caring little about those who we hurt along the way. Read over the following list and ask yourself if you've done any any of these or similar things.

Have you ever:

- Stolen from someone who trusted you?
- Borrowed money you never paid back?
- Crashed at a friend or family member's house without contributing, even knowing their finances were stretched thin?
- Neglected to pay bills in order to get high, despite the fact that others depended on you?
- Neglected your children?
- Asked for money while locked up to "buy food or hygiene" then spent it on drugs?
- Taken advantage of a woman for what she could do for you?
- Lied to your family or friends?

In Ásatrú we have a name for actions of this type. We call it "breaking frith." But before you go any further down the path of hospitality, it's important to fully understand the concept of frith.

Frith

First let me say, with all honesty, that I personally do not believe that we today are able to understand the depths of frith as our ancestors lived it. To them, frith was as natural and inviolable as the need to breathe. When we read the sagas and see examples of how frith could rise up and tear a man's life apart, we are amazed at his strength of character and loyalty toward his kinsman. What we fail to realize is that he could not do otherwise. The dictates of his society would not allow it.

Back then, frith was hardcore. Imagine living in a tightknit community. From the day you're born, everyone around you is either blood or distant kin. This is a true Inangard. Your success is their success; their success is your success. You may not like everyone, you may not agree with everyone, but you will never turn against them. Any outside threat against the individual is a threat against the whole and will be dealt with accordingly. Whether the individual was right or wrong is secondary to the Inangard's protection.

Gronbech says, "All must give way to frith, all obligations, all considerations of self, everything down to the regard for one's personal dignity; if such a thing could be imagined as existing apart from the feeling of kinship... Frith is the state of things which exists between friends. And it means, first and foremost, reciprocal inviolability. However individual wills may clash in a conflict of kin against kin, however stubbornly individual heads may seek their own way according to their quota of wisdom, there can never be question of conflict save in the sense of thoughts and feelings working their way toward an equipoise in unity."

This pure concept of frith was diluted over the years by the rise of the state as law and order, and a more individualistic society. In some circles it has disappeared entirely with the "every man for himself" mindset. As Ásatrúar, the success or failure of our Great Awakening will depend on to what degree we can revive the concept of frith within the constraints of the modern world.

In the Seeds of Oak Hofguild we emphasize the importance of frith. Our Rede reflect this. The very first law states, "No one shall break the frith of our hall for any reason, at any time." Members will seethe with anger or walk out of group before they break frith in the hall. Another law advises guests to frith-build at every opportunity. Several times a year, someone will give a presentation on frith for new guests. We teach frith as a synonym for trust, goodwill, friendship, and peace. Frith is our rally cry when brothers engage in negativity, bickering and gossip.

But what happens when someone breaks frith? Usually, if the person is new to this way of life they will try to apologize. Elder Ásatrúar know better. Apologies are words, and words are wind. When we're in the wrong, we make amends.

Which leads us to wergild.

Wergild

Traditionally wergild meant "man payment". Everyone in society, from the lowest thrall, to the highest jarl had a monetary value assigned to them. If you killed someone, and the victim's family was inclined to peace, then you could pay wergild and be absolved of the crime. But if the family didn't accept wergild (and the further back you go, they rarely did) this would lead to a blood feud that could rage for generations.

This system may seem savage and archaic to most modern men. But if they could look at things objectively, they would see that the system survives to this very day, albeit in a civilized pretense. The court systems are now the ones who issue wergild in the form of fines or prison sentences. In violent crimes the victim's families are often given a voice in whether or not a deal is given. And for some crimes society agrees that no amount of fines or incarceration is enough and the perpetrator must pay in blood. The only difference is the State enacts the death penalty, not the victim's family, although they are allowed to watch.

And if the idea that certain people should be worth more than others is repugnant to you, if you feel like in modern times all men are created equal, all I can say is, rob a crackhead and rob a congressman and see which gets you more time.

In the Seeds of Oak we try not to view wergild as punishment, so much as it is an atonement. When someone commits a nid, this pits them against the community. Wergild is how they once again become "at one" with the community. The wergild varies in severity based on the nid. Something small like cursing in the hall costs a stamp. Failing to follow through on a commitment costs a workout or a presentation. For a serious nid, such as lying on a brother, einviggi, or one on one combat, might be the only acceptable wergild. What all of these nids have in common is that once wergild is paid, the nid is forgotten as if it never even happened. The balance has been paid, so there's no throwing it in the person's face later on.

On the Path of Hospitality you are asked to make a list of all the people whom you have broken frith with during your addiction. Next to each person's name write a brief description of how you've wronged them. Then you need to contact each person and explain that

47

you're genuinely seeking recovery. Admit that you've wronged them in the past and want to make amends. Tell them you don't believe in apologies and would rather do something to show your sincerity. Let them set the terms of wergild. Maybe they'll ask you to help them with household chores, or maybe they'll ask you to stay out of their life. Whatever it is, once you accept it, you are honor-bound to follow through.

But what if there are circumstances in which wergild is impossible? It could be you were a deadbeat dad and your child can no longer be a part of your life. You can't consider child support wergild because that is already your responsibility as a father. But maybe you could be there for another child, a niece or nephew, or a child in the Big Brother program.

Or maybe someone whom you wronged has passed away. You will never be able to make it up to them in person, but there are other ways. You can look after their family, honor them during sumble, or donate money to their favorite charity. Wyrd connects us all, and positive acts reverberate across the web.

The process of wergild is dynamic. It's beneficial to the person you broke frith with and to you. The person you wronged can see that you recognize your transgression and respect them enough to make amends. For you, it works towards clearing your hamingja or personal luck.

Picture your life as a tapestry. During the years of drug abuse, poor decisions snagged and tangled all the threads into a chaotic mess. Now you are consciously untangling the threads. While you can't change the pattern that has already been laid down - those snags will always be there - you can ensure that the thread you're laying now is free of tangles.

And now that your hamingja is getting stronger you will notice that, more and more often, things seem to go your way. It's not magic. When you have a positive mindset, take responsibility for your actions, and respect others, you will attract circumstances that reflect your higher evolution. You are now ready for the next Path.

Matt's Saga

Matt was finishing a set of pushups when his phone rang. An automated voice said it was a call from Augusta Correctional Center. *Strange to be on the other side of one of these calls,* he thought as he hit one to accept.

"Hello?"

"Heilsa. Don't tell me you've only been gone a few months and already forgot how to greet a bro."

Hearing Ryland's voice took a weight off Matt's shoulders because it meant he'd kept his word. He had wondered if Ryland got the email with his new number. Ryland was the goði of the kindred at Augusta, the man who'd introduced him to Asatru. Ryland was an Odinist who insisted that all his brothers focus on bettering themselves through education and trades. Matt could remember countless nights they'd spun laps around the rec yard, as Ryland patiently explained some aspect of the faith.

At that moment Matt realized how much he missed the discipline and frith they all had. And while he didn't miss prison, he damn sure missed some of the people.

For the next twenty minutes Matt told Ryland everything that had happened since his release. It felt good to have someone he trusted and respected to confide in. Before he knew it, the operator gave them the one minute warning.

This time when Ryland called back Matt thought to ask him how things were going with the kindred.

"Same old, same old. Right now we're getting ready for Yule. I'm pushing paper to make sure the Administration doesn't screw us over again."

"I wish I could be there."

"Let's trade places then," Ryland joked.

Matt laughed. There was a long pause. Then he said, "Listen bro... I just wanted to say I'm sorry it took so long to reach out."

"Don't apologize. When you're wrong, you make amends."

"If you want wergild, name it. I get paid Friday and can send the group some books."

"We're good right now, but I'll keep that in mind. I have a better idea. Now that you're on your feet, it's time to work on your hamingja. I want you to make a list of all the people you've broken frith with and make it right."

Matt rubbed his temples. How much easier it would've been to just write a check. But this was his goði, and while he never let him take the easy way out, he never steered him wrong either.

"Alright, I'll do it. But it's going to be a long list."

The Path of Perseverance

There are few better examples of perseverance than Eirik the Red.

His saga begins with violence. The saga writer, in typical Scandinavian stoicism, states that he and his father sailed to Iceland because they'd been involved in slayings.

His wild ways continued there. After marrying Thjodhild, he cleared land and built a farm. His slaves just so happened to cause a landslide that took out a rival farmstead. Coincidence? Possibly. But the farmer's kinsman Filth-Eyjolf didn't think so. He killed all the slaves. Eirik answered back by killing Filth-Eyjolf and his buddy, Hrafn the Dueler.

Seeing that blood revenge wasn't working out too well for them, Eyjolf's kinsman sought redress at the Thing for his killing. The Thing decided to outlaw Eirik the Red from Iceland, eager to get such a wild man out of the community.

Eirik respected the Thing's decision and packed up and moved to an island off the coast. While there, he lent a man named Thorgest bedstead boards. For some reason, when it came time to return the boards, Thorgest refused. So Eirik went and took them. When Thorgest found out, he went after Eirik and got two of his sons killed for his effort.

Once again, Eirik was sentenced to outlawry and exiled. There weren't many places he could still go to, so he announced that he would search for the land that Gunnbjorn had spotted when he was driven off course westward. After avoiding Thorgest's ships who were still trying to kill him, he set out over the empty ocean, for a rumor of land.

The Goðin smiled on Eirik because he found the land. Or maybe they were laughing because the land was almost uninhabitable, an island of huge glaciers and frozen tundra. As Eirik surveyed the land, giving names to different sites, he knew that he couldn't settle there alone. He could've given up. Instead, in one of the earliest recorded cases of false advertising, he named the island Greenland, thinking that more people would be attracted there if it had an inviting name. He was right.

The sagas don't go into detail about the problems Eirik the Red overcame settling Greenland. It's probable that the daily struggles inherent to building a thriving society in this wasteland eclipsed everything he'd been through so far. And that's not even taking into consideration the family issues he was plagued with.

Eirik was a heathen and worshipped the Goðin of his ancestors. However, his son Leif became a vassal of Olaf "the Traitor" Tryggvasson and pledged to convert Greenland to Christianity. This had to bother Eirik, especially since his wife was one of the first to convert. But Eirik followed the old ways and suffered in silence rather than break frith with his family. The only sign that he hated the new religion was when he made his wife build her church far from their house so he wouldn't hear the bleating of her prayers.

A normal man, having accomplished all that Eirik had, would retire and settle into a peaceful old age. But Eirik never grew complacent, never stopped striving. When his son asked him to lead one last voyage to the west, claiming that Eirik still commanded the greatest good fortune of his kinsmen, the old heathen wasn't hard to convince. He buried his gold and made ready to leave. If he hadn't injured himself falling off his horse, he would've helped discover Vinland.

Tru Grit

At any point, Eirik the Red could have given up. He could've listened to everyone who said he was an outlaw, skulked off to some island and disappeared from history. But because of his uncommon resolve and perseverance, we know who he is today.

Perseverance is having the grit to follow through with your goals no matter what obstacles arise. It's accepting that failure is not an option. That's not to say that failure doesn't happen, it just happens to other people. When you view every obstacle as trial and error, and vow to keep trying despite any setbacks, you literally can't fail. You might not have succeeded yet, but you haven't failed either.

How do you respond to obstacles? Do you give up, make excuses, or point to the next man's shortcomings, or do you find a way to adapt and overcome? If you want to build perseverance, do less of the former and more of the latter. Never suggest that something is impossible and once you commit to something, see it through no matter what.

As Ásatrúar, we want men around us with perseverance. We want to know they'll stand beside us when times are hard. We look at forging perseverance like forging a sword; the sword isn't strong despite the Hammer and the fire, but because of them.

The Heilræðr of the Seed of Oak, Bryan Stevens, is an example of what perseverance can accomplish. He had a rough time coming up in the Hofguild. He was given the hardest presentations, the most grueling workouts, and the shit jobs that no one wanted to do. No one held his hand or complimented him for a job well done. In fact, some guys probably wanted to see him fail. But you know what? He now holds the second highest position in the Hofguild, while so many other guys have fallen off.

A scene from Fight Club always comes to mind when I think of perseverance. Two guy shows up on Brad Pitt and Edward Norton's doorstep trying to join their anarchist movement. They tell one guy he can't join and he shrugs his shoulders and leaves. The other guy stands there for days. They scream at him to leave, tell him he's worthless. They compliment him but say he's not what they're looking for. Throughout it all he stands there, stoically. Only after he's proven his perseverance do they let him inside.

Which guy are you, the one who gives up after the first setback, or the Asa-man who will shake his fist at the Goðin if they get in his way?

Perseverance and Addiction

If you've walked the previous Paths, it's obvious that you possess an amount of perseverance. There's no way you could've made it this far without it. But now that the most urgent part of your recovery is behind you, it's more necessary than ever to guard against complacency.

There will be days when sobriety feels like the most natural thing in the world and you never even think about drugs. Then there will be days when thoughts of getting high are stuck in your head like a bad song and it takes every ounce of willpower not to give in. And there's no telling what type of day you'll wake up to.

For many addicts, the period when they've been clean for some time and have grown accustomed to sobriety is a dangerous time. It's all too easy to tell yourself that you've beaten your addiction. Thoughts like this can cause you to loosen up, let your discipline slip. "I'm fine," you tell yourself. "It won't hurt to get high once a month. But once a month turns into only on the weekends which turns into a full blown habit.

Whatever you do, don't give in. I promise you the temporary pleasure isn't worth how defeated you'll feel to be back where you started.

What you need is a strategy to deal with these urges when they arise. 3-D habit change is that strategy. I can't take credit for it. Mighty heils to Friederike Fabritius and Hans Hagemann of the Munich Leadership Group.

3-D habit change is a three step process of describe, distract, and delay.

Describe: The first step in fighting the urge is to recognize and acknowledge it. A big part of the hold these urges have over us is the ability to operate subconsciously. By exposing the urge to your conscious thought, you've found a chink in the armor and given yourself a fighting chance.

Once you've acknowledged the urge, describe it aloud to yourself. "I just got off from work. It's Friday, and this is the time when I used to cash my check and cop a bag. I want to get high." Or, "I've had a few beers and now I want to sniff some coke."

Describing what you're thinking gives you a chance to exert conscious control over an unconscious response.

Distract: Trying to go heads up with the urge to get high is not the most effective strategy. Your brain has already anticipated the pleasure and will view anything less as punishment. The brain doesn't take kindly to punishment. Resisting an urge directly is more likely to make it worse. It's like telling you not to think about pink elephants; suddenly it's all you can think about. So it's better to redirect the energy to something else. Instead of getting high, eat some candy, listen to music, or look at porn. The best distractions are ones that give the brain a small dose of what it wants.

Delay: Once you've found a way to beat the urge, you have to sustain it. The more often you use the positive behavior to offset the negative, the more ingrained it becomes. The two habits will fight for supremacy, but eventually, with enough repetition, the new habit will overcome the old one as new neuronal pathways are developed. Think of it like you're slowly redirecting a flow of water into a new channel. Over time, the old channel will dry up.

The Path of Perseverance is one you will continue to walk for a long time to come. But it's because of the brain's ability to change that I don't believe the old adage "Once an addict, always an addict." With perseverance, there will come a day when the fetters of drug addiction no longer hold you prisoner.

Now let's continue on to the next Path.

Matt's Saga

One night, when the urge to get high had him crawling out of his skin, Matt decided to go to a meeting.

The one he attended was in the back of an old Bingo hall. Fluorescent lights cast a haggard glow on the people inside. He grabbed a Styrofoam cup of stale coffee and found a seat in the far back corner.

The meeting reminded him of the first time he'd attended blot. He felt lost as the secretary read from the laminated cards and the rest of the group responded in a dull monotone. They looked at him, blinking, when he said his name was Matt until he added uncertainly, "And I'm an addict?"

"Hi, Matt."

Ironically, the step they were discussing that night was submitting to a higher power. Despite the New Age euphemisms it was obvious that the Christian god was intended. Matt couldn't help but smile as he thought of asking Odin to take away his burdens. The Allfather would send a few more burdens his way just to teach perseverance.

The meeting went downhill from there. During open discussion, person after person described the details of their addictions. An air of despair filled the room and Matt sensed that many took a masochistic pleasure in trying to one-up the depths they'd sunk to. The greatest sympathy was reserved for those who'd recently relapsed, reinforcing the defeatist mentality.

As the meeting drew to a close, Matt eyed the exit. When they circled up for the Serenity Prayer he made his move. He wasn't much of a hugger.

Stepping into the cool night air, Matt tugged the collar of his Carhart up to his chin. He expected his shitty mood to return, but to his surprise, he felt great. It wasn't because of the meeting, either. While NA and AA had helped many people, he knew it wasn't for him. He wouldn't be coming back.

No, what cheered him up was the knowledge that the lessons he'd learned in Ásatrú group had taken root in his life. He wasn't a powerless thrall begging for Divine mercy. No matter what the world threw at him, he knew the power to handle it dwelt inside him. No matter what he would persevere.

The Path of Self-Reliance

"Why so hard?" the kitchen coal once said to the diamond. "After all, are we not close kin?"
Why so soft? O my brothers, thus I ask you: Are you not after all my brothers?
Why so soft, so pliant and yielding? Why is there so much denial, self-denial, in your hearts? So little destiny in your eyes?
And if you do not want to be destinies and inexorable ones, how can you triumph with me?
And if your hardness does not wish to flash and cut through, how can you one day create with me?

Nietzsche

If the previous Paths have led you through the dark woods of addiction, the Path of Self-Reliance is where you break the treeline and can see the sun on the horizon. Before, you've had to focus on your past and present in order to get your bearings. Now you can finally begin to see the possibilities of the future. On this Path you will stop looking at yourself as just an addict, and will instead begin to identify what your tru purpose is.

But first you will have to figure out what is most important in life. Let's see what our lore has to say.

The Three Wells

It is not often remembered that the Goðin were not always the rulers of the nine worlds. At one time, during the primal age, Ymir and the fearsome brood born of his feet were the ones in power. The Goðin, the Norns, and the members of the noble Jötun race dwelled in a peaceful section of Jormungrund.

Odin was not content to live at the whim of another. Although young and inexperienced, he knew that he was destined for great things. So one day he climbed to the top of the world-tree and surveyed the lands he knew in his heart rightfully belonged to him. He looked down on Ymir and the Jötun race with disgust.

Everywhere they went, chaos followed. Odin knew that he would have to rid the world of these monsters before he could fulfill his other duties. War was inevitable.

Those who are familiar with this story, know what happened next. Odin sacrificed himself for a sip from Mímir's Well. But let us put ourselves in his shoes for a moment. Why did he choose to risk his life for a sip from this well, when there we're two other wells to choose from?

The mead from Hvergelmir is called Svalkaldur Saær and it grants endurance to anyone who drinks from it. This had to be tempting to Odin who was about to go to war. With one sip, he could guarantee that he would outlast his foes. He would ensure his own survival. But this could lead to a long, drawn-out war that would lay waste to the world. And Odin didn't simply want to survive, he wanted to prosper. So he did not sip from this well.

Then there's Urðarbrunnr whose mead, Urðar Magn, gives strength and power to whoever drinks from it. This, too, must've tempted Odin. The terror he would strike on the battlefield! No Jötun would be able to stand against him. Not many people would be able to pass up the temptation of this well. But Odin knew that wars are long and one warrior cannot win by strength of arm alone. Or, maybe he knew deep down, that by valuing power and strength above all else, he would be no better than his enemy. Whatever his reason, Odin did not drink from this well, either.

As it turned out, Odin chose to risk his life for a sip from Mímirsbrunnr, whose mead grants wisdom. He knew that wisdom, above all, would help him to win the war. Wisdom would give him the foresight to see through his enemies' plans and to counter them with his own. Wisdom would show him when to be patient and endure; wisdom would show him when to be fierce and attack with strength. Therefore, a sip from this well was like a sip from all three.

War, when it came, was quick and brutal. Ymir slew Audhumla with his insatiable hunger, and in return, Odin and his brothers slew Ymir. They hacked into his neck. Blood surged from the wound, drowning the rest of the monstrous Jötnar except for one.

The war was over almost as quick as it began. Now Odin and his brothers were faced with the question of what to do next. Here again, Odin's choice to sip from the well of wisdom proved beneficial. Even amongst all the death and destruction, he was fully aware of his life task. He would be a Creator.

Self-Realization

There are two ways to look at self-reliance. The first way is the exoteric and it involves being able to depend on yourself to meet whatever challenges may arise in everyday life. An Ásatrúar should be able to change a tire, set a budget, keep his environment clean, perform a blot, give a heil, respect the beliefs of others while defending his own, cook the perfect steak, comfort a sick child, throw a punch, take a punch, act alone or in a group, read a tape measure or a poem, sit with the dying, show grace under pressure, bait a hook, setup a campsite, honor his elders, enjoy solitude in nature, make a woman feel loved and secure, live bravely and die courageously. In short, be a man among men.

The second way to look at self-reliance is more esoteric. It involves realizing that you, and only you, have the power to affect your spiritual evolution. We are put here on Midgard to learn and transcend. Our actions determine which Hall we inhabit after death, and our future birth. If you consciously decide to act, this will happen. If you do not consciously decide to act, but drift with the current, this will still happen. Choosing not to decide is still a decision.

What spiritual seeker in his right mind would leave this to chance? If your spiritual evolution or spiritual descent are inevitable, wouldn't it be better to take control of the process? The only things holding most people back are fear and ignorance. People are afraid to take control over their evolution, because if they fail, there's no one to blame but themselves. Unfortunately, this is something they will have to face alone. No one can help them through this "dark night of the soul".

But for us Ásatrúar, ignorance should never be an excuse. The Goðin and our ancestors have laid the path for us to follow to transcendence. Our lore is filled with shining examples for those with eyes to see. The stories of Starkad and Sigurd depict the perfect Odinnic hero. The story of Odr shows how one man reached godhood. Like all great myths, they are filled with occult symbolism.

A more recent example of someone who lives the godly life is the the goði. The goði, which means "he who speaks with the godly tongue", was part priest, and part politician. This harkens back to the Golden Age when the King and Priest were the same man, able to trace his lineage back to Odin. As the Nordic saying goes, "May our leader be our bridge." These early kings embodied an earthly divinity which filled their people with awe. It was the reason they were venerated and obeyed (and sometimes sacrificed when crops failed).

While the goði didn't hold the power of a king, he did hold a prominent role in Scandinavian society. His wisdom and insight was seen to be a gift from the Goðin, and he was often called to settle disputes among the Folk.

But to call the goði's wisdom a "gift" is misleading. He had to work for it. There was an initiatic process the goði had to undergo to make himself worthy of the gift. A passage from the Hugrunar gives a practical explanation of this process. Here I will attempt to explain what each step entails in order to give a better understanding of how you can apply it to your personal evolution.

"Seven years before the wind a captain makes. Eight steps makes the goði."

"First, hear of the old ones, know what has gone before." This is your foundation as you study history, learn the lore, and listen to your elders. This step takes humility to admit that you don't have all the answers, but by standing on the shoulders of those who've gone before, you can reach greater heights. This is intellectual knowledge, and while it is important, it's only the first step. There are still deeper ways to gain knowledge and insight.

"Second, seek solitude in quiet, green places to prove runar." At some point you have to learn how to apply this newfound knowledge to your life. Knowledge without thought is useless. Only by spending time alone, contemplating your place in the world and the natural laws (runes) of existence, can you proceed further.

"Third journey foodless, sleepless, past the world of men, and seek quiet moment for the voice of Goðin." This is the level of supraconsciousness, where you directly experience the Goðin. Our ancestors believed that certain shamanic practices such as fasting from food or sleep made one more receptive to altered states of awareness. This is the concept of ansuz, or divine inspiration.

The Asatru Edda leaves out the fourth step in the Hugrunar. I don't know if this is intentional or not.

Moving on…

"Act as seer, warrior, caster of the stones of Wyrd, as healer, or as scribe." This is one of the most important steps on the Path of Self-Reliance. What do all of these professions have in common? The one similarity between them is that they don't take anything from the community. All they do is give. A seer and rune vitki give guidance. A healer gives hope, a scribe knowledge. A warrior gives protection and his life if necessary. It's obvious that our ancestors viewed the higher man as one who selflessly worked to uplift the Folk.

"Reach and bring another to the Thing, goðord to train." A time will come when the next generation looks to you for guidance. As someone helped to show you the way, it's your duty to do the same.

"To the world of men apply the Thing-spoken wisdom." As you walk this path and live with virtue, people will naturally look to you for advice and to settle disputes. Always strive to be just.

"Learn and live the herder's stone hut and the crossroads of men, at once in both, and speak the Thing." This line is a riddle which reveals itself with a little thought. The herder's stone hut means living in solitude, away from people. The crossroads of men means being in the thick of things. How can we live in both at once? This simply addresses a tendency of mystics to want to retreat into their solitude. But we're not meant to escape into some cave like a hermit. We are to live and experience all that life has to offer; that is the crossroads of men. The herder's stone hut is our mind. We may live physically in the mundane world even as we distance ourselves by thinking godly thoughts and speaking godly words.

These are the steps the goði must walk during his initiation. They are the same steps I'm asking you to walk on the Path of Self-Reliance. I no longer want you to identify yourself as an addict. You are a child of the Goðin. Every possibility that exists in them, exists in you. It's time to claim your birthright as an Ásaman and identify your Life Task.

Uncovering Your Life Task

One of the saddest things in the world is wasted potential. As an Odinist, I would rather see someone fail miserably doing something they love, than settle for something they don't. I spend a lot of time trying to get my brothers to identify what they're passionate about, because once you can do this, the rest of life becomes easy. The saying "Do something you love and you'll never work a day in your life", has a lot of truth to it.

Sadly very few Ásatrúar are able to articulate their Life Task. So many drift into their forties and fifties without a clear sense of direction. There are a variety of reasons why this is so. Some are worried about what others might think. (They should be more worried that genius and conformity rarely mix.) Some simply never take the time to consider the question. And some view money as a better measure of success than challenge and fulfillment.

This last one is prevalent in today's society. A brother of mine is, hands down, the best artist I've ever known. When he sits down and takes his time with a drawing, the results are amazing. With his level of talent, it's impossible for him not to love what he does. But slowly I'm seeing that love disappear. We've spoken about it, and he says it comes from having to work on projects he doesn't enjoy. Easy stuff like cards and handkerchiefs. I can't draw a stick figure and even I can see it's because these projects don't challenge him. I've recommended that he work on something big, a masterpiece that pushes him to the edge of his talent and beyond. "Yeah, but work like that doesn't pay the bills. I gotta eat."

A part of me gets it. We all have to deal with the realities of life. But beyond the necessities of food, clothing, and shelter, it's all extracurricular. And that's why a bigger part of me will never get it. A part of me will always be an idealist. My heart goes out to those who are willing to suffer for their convictions, to starve for their art, to die for a just cause. These are the heroic men and women whom we never tire hearing stories about.

Now let's take a look at your Life Task. (Don't get hung up on the wording; it can be used interchangeably with Purpose, Chief Aim, or Great Work.) I want you to contemplate your own uniqueness and what sets you apart from others. When the Norns laid out your wyrd, it was like no one else's. During the times in your life when you listened to your inner voice, (which I believe is the fylgja) you were acting in line with your deepest yearnings. Times like these you probably remember to be lucky and fulfilling, like you could overcome any obstacle. But when you ignored this voice, you felt the exact opposite: Burdened, unlucky and powerless. By identifying your Life Task you make the conscious decision to always listen to and trust your fylgja.

The following personal questions will help you define your Life Task. Try not to force the answers or intellectualize. Above all, don't base your answers on what someone else wants. Your own insight is what truly matters.

- What unique skills do you have that set you apart from the herd?
- What do you do that puts you in a flow state, and makes hours seem like minutes?
- If money wasn't an issue, what would you do?
- What virtues or principles are important to you? Does your current lifestyle reflect these ideals?
- What have *others* told you that you are supposed to do with your life?
- What do *you* think you are supposed to do with your life?
- If you had to attend your own funeral, what do you think people would say? What would you *want* them to say?

Take the answers to these questions and in a few sentences, write out your Life Task. Just by completing this important step, you are farther ahead than 90% of the world. But it's not enough to simply know your life's task; now you have to live it.

Matt's Saga

"I'm offering you a promotion. It'll mean working nights again, but the pay will be better."

Matt crunched the ice in his water, stalling for time. He'd known this offer was coming. His boss, a middle-aged Irish man named Mr. Brighton, had taken a liking to him. He was always on time and could fill in at any position, from cook to bar back. He'd even broken up a couple fights without having to hurt anybody. Now that he was clean, Matt found he was a good worker.

Problem was, he wasn't sure this was the job he wanted. Working around alcohol constantly tested his sobriety. Not to mention, it was a rare shift when someone didn't ask him to get them some cocaine, as if a tattooed neck and sleeves guaranteed he had a connect. One time a bachelorette party cornered him by the pool tables and shoved a rolled-up bill in his hand. And that was a day shift. Nights would be even worse, especially if Mr. Brighton had him running security for the strip club, too.

"I need to take some time to think about it," he replied.

"Sure. Let me know something by the weekend."

During the drive back to the motel, Matt considered his options. This wasn't the first job offer he'd received this week. An old friend wanted him to come work at a new bike shop he was opening up. The pay wouldn't be that great at first, but there was nowhere to go but up. Plus, it would give him the opportunity to put the trade he'd learned in prison, small engine repair, to good use.

Matt stopped by Zero's Sub Shop for a grinder and a salad before heading to the motel. He paid up for another week, waved to the maid, and went to his room.

After a quick shower, Matt sat down to eat. Suddenly he had an idea. He would do a rune pull in the hope of shedding some light on his problem. It had been a long time since he'd done one. He hoped he wasn't too out of practice.

First things first, he performed a blot to Odin as bringer of the runes. For the sacrifice he placed a portion of the grinder in the bowli. It was no freshly killed pig, but Matt was sure Odin would appreciate Genoa salami and Cappicola ham.

Next, Matt laid down a pillowcase for his altar cloth and took out his rune set. He had personally carved and blooded them years ago. Then he calmed his mind. Once he was completely focused he asked the question: "Which job should I accept?" So there would be no confusion, he pictured himself working each job in his mind's eye.

Once this was done, he reached in the bag. Some Ásatrúar preferred to actually cast the runes, but he liked to touch them all until one felt "right".

He selected three runes and set them down on the cloth without looking at them. He took a deep breath and focused on the reading. His view on the runes was that they helped you connect with your Higher Self. Therefore it was important to go with your gut response. Too much intellectualizing could cloud the reading.

The first rune was ansuz. He always took this rune to mean something that was inspiring. What inspired him? The only thing he could think of was his art. He could spend hours drawing and it would seem like only minutes had passed. But it was hard to see how this could apply to either job.

The second rune was berkano. He always equated this rune with women. There would be plenty of women at the strip club and he knew he wouldn't like watching white women be degraded onstage like that. But he didn't think this was the significance of the pull. It didn't feel right. Maybe it signified a woman in his life who meant something to him? The shop job would be more stable...

The last rune was fehu. He had to flip it right side up because it was in the murkstave position. The negative side of money and wealth. He felt like the runes were telling him not to choose a job just because it pays a little more.

He decided to take the shop job. He couldn't explain it, but it felt right. Not wasting any time, he called his buddy and told him the good news.

"I'm glad you called. I was beginning to think I'd have to hire someone else."

"I really want the job, but there's one favor I need to ask."

"If it's about the money, I really can't go any higher. This is gonna be a bootstrap operation for the first year or so."

"It's not about the money. I know you're hiring me as a mechanic, but in my spare time I want to try my hand at airbrushing and fabrication."

"That's it? No problem. And I'll tell you what; if you show any type of talent, I'll even send you to school for it."

Smiling, Matt hung up the phone already planning his two week notice.

The Path of Honor

Even the Goðin can lose their honor. Odin learned this the hard way.

After slaying the third incarnation of Gullveig, Odin was put on trial at the Folkvig. The Vanir accused him of spilling the witch's blood in a holy place, without considering her kinship ties to Frey. They demanded wergild that Odin, in good conscience, could not pay. Odin would have paid it, but he understood the precedent it would set. It would show mankind that he thought it was a crime to execute an enemy of the Goðin, responsible for spreading seiðr throughout Midgard.

While this was a valid argument, it ultimately proved his undoing. The Vanir pointed out the hypocrisy of condemning seiðr when Odin himself had practiced it on occasion. They gave as an example the time he had seduced Rind using a magic potion. In the end, they decided that Odin had tarnished his honor and must be exiled.

Odin was enraged. A schism grew between the Goðin as the Æsir and Vanir took sides. The natural order of the world was threatened by the possibility of war. If Odin and the other Goðin of war had attacked, their victory was likely. But it would have come at too great a cost. Odin always had one eye on Ragnarok, and he could see that the Goðin must stand united if they were to prevail against Surtr.

So Odin heeded Mímir's counsel, which was to barricade himself in Asgard. The Æsir should defend themselves if attacked, but stop short of killing the Vanir. If somehow the Vanir managed to breach their defenses, Odin should retreat rather than kill his former comrades. There would be no dishonor in such a retreat; in fact, it was the only chance to one day regain the frith that had been lost.

The war began and for a while it appeared to be a stalemate. Try as they might, the Vanir could not breach Asgard's wall. But then Njord had the ingenious plan to capture Sleipnir and leap into the courtyard. After that it was a simple matter to smash the gate with his mighty battle-axe. His warriors streamed into the fortress.

True to his intentions, Odin surrendered Asgard to prevent unnecessary bloodshed. He took the ultimate walk of shame, stripped of his titles, his godhood, and outlawed. The Vanir had no other choice. They had to make an example of him lest all of his followers think that such inappropriate behavior was acceptable. Eventually, people would grow ashamed of the Goðin.

Dishonored, Odin went into exile. Imagine his shame. His wife Frigga had left him and was sleeping with his brothers. Ullr now sat on his throne and was even being called Odin. Everything he had worked so hard to build was crumbling around him. The Mighty had fallen and he had no one to blame but himself.

A lesser man would have become bitter. How much easier it would have been to blame his circumstances on Gullveig, the faithless Vanir, or wyrd. But Odin faced adversity with nobility and wisdom.

Then, out of nowhere, an opportunity arose for Odin to regain his throne. The Jötnar asked Odin to ally with them against the Vanir. Once they were victorious, they would allow him to rule in Asgard.

But Odin did not compound his crimes with such a dishonorable act. He would not endanger mankind and his former comrades for his own ambition. He warned the Vanir and helped them fight the Jötnar. So many Jötnar were killed that they will not recover their numbers until shortly before Ragnarok.

After the battle, the Æsir and Vanir remembered the frith they once shared. Odin's selfless act had paved the way for a reconciliation, and time had done the rest. The Vanir felt that Odin had suffered enough and restored him to his former glory.

The Ásatrú Edda states, "Once Odin had recovered his divine regalia, he shone throughout the earth with such lustrous renown that all peoples welcomed him like a light returned to the universe. There was nowhere in the entire globe which did not pay homage to his sacred power. He banished the seiðr as his first act and dispersed the groups of its practitioners which had sprung up, like shadows before the oncoming of his sacred brightness."

It seems that a god can lose his honor, but he can also regain it. I think it's a testament to our way of life that our Goðin are held to the same standards we are.

What is Honor?

Honor is a concept that the average person doesn't give much thought to. The word itself sounds archaic. Looking around it's hard to believe that, for most of history, men's lives revolved around their honor. To be dishonored, especially in a warrior society, was to be cast out, ignored, viewed as less than a man.

Our ancestors had a deep sense of honor. The slightest insult could have severe repercussions because men were willing to die for their honor. And if they were slow to avenge an insult, often the women around them would goad them into action. It was understood that honor was sacred to the individual and the community as a whole.

And it's not like in modern times, where the higher a man's station, the more untouchable he seems. You see it all the time now, CEOs and politicians acting without any respect for right and wrong and never being punished. Or if they are punished, it's only a slap on the wrist. In Viking society, the higher a man rose, the further he had to fall, and therefore he had to be even more protective of his honor. According to Gronbech, "It touched the chieftain's personal honour, his honour as a man, if he failed to devote all his energies to the fulfillment of such obligations as went with his position. He had not an official honour to spend first; if he failed to live up to his duties as a leader of men, his chieftainship sank at once to nidinghood, without stopping on the way at the stage of ordinary respectability."

To our ancestors, honor wasn't something that could be picked up or set aside when it suited you. Their concept of honor was more hardcore than we're used to. It may even be impossible for us to live up to such a standard. But the difference between them and us is that they were raised in a society in which the rules of honor were clearly understood. We, on the other hand, are trying to reawaken our sense of honor in a sick and decadent society.

The question of honor is especially hard to answer in prison, or in a community of addicts. It's nearly impossible to find an Ásatrúar who has never sacrificed his honor at some point. How could we not, when we were never told how valuable it is? So you do the best you can. In the Seeds of Oak, we draw the line with certain nids, such as sex crimes and victimizing women and children. And for the others, we give them the benefit of the doubt, teach them how to live by virtue, and then hold them to a higher standard.

But back to the original topic... what is honor? To me, honor is different than the other virtues because you can't practice honor. It is a state of being; either you are honorable, or you are not. It is the sum total of how well you are living the other eight virtues.

And since you cannot practice honor, there is nothing you must do on this path. This is a time to celebrate. Look back at how far you have come and take pride in regaining your honor. Mighty heils! You've earned it.

Donning Your Hammer

If on the Path of Truth you decided to take off your Hammer while you worked the steps, then now is the time to return it to its rightful place. But don't simply put it back on. I would recommend you take the time to design a ritual that shows how sacred this moment is. Bury your Hammer in the ground for nine nights before a Black Moon. Nine is a holy number, and the Black Moon, or New Moon, is an auspicious time for new beginnings. This will help sanctify your Hammer. When you do put in on, perform a blot to your fultru and recommit yourself to the Goðin.

Matt's Saga

Matt carefully picked his steps as he followed an old game trail through the woods. The stars shining through skeletal branches were all he had to light his way. He had chosen tonight because it was a Black Moon, the best time for new beginnings.

The trail wasn't entirely unfamiliar. He had walked it nine days ago, searching for an appropriate place to bury his Hammer.

The purpose of burying his Hammer was to clear any negative hamingja associated with it. He had gotten the idea from his goði. When they were at Augusta, a brother had allowed someone to smack him and didn't retaliate. Ryland called a Thing and took his Hammer for being a coward. They would've destroyed it, but back then Hammers were hard to come by, so they buried it on the Yard for nine nights.

Matt didn't want to destroy his Hammer either. It was the first and only one he had ever worn, and it had sentimental value because of the brothers who donned it on him. So he'd scouted out this place in Pungo and buried it nine days ago.

But none of that would matter if he couldn't find the place. He was beginning to worry he might have to come back with a flashlight, or even worse, when the sun was out.

Suddenly, he emerged from the treeline into a small clearing shaped like a perfect circle. Pine needles rustled beneath his boots. Otherwise, the night was silent. It was all too easy to imagine he'd been transported back to a time before the rise of Christianity, when his ancestors worshipped beneath star and sky.

At the far side of the clearing stood a majestic oak. Many lesser trees had to die for it to rise to such heights. As soon as Matt had laid eyes on it, he knew it was a positive omen. His fultru was Thor and the oak was sacred to him.

Now Matt crouched down and dug in the earth beneath the roots. The top layer was nearly frozen, but as he dug deeper, the soil loosened to a rich, black loam. Before long, his hand struck metal.

Carefully, so the chain didn't snag on a root, Matt retrieved his Hammer. He dusted the dirt from its surface, the silver gleaming in the starlight. Was it just his imagination, or did it feel purified?

About that time his phone rang. He and Ryland had set up a time to call, and that's who it was. He could hear a few of the brothers in Ryland's pod talking in the background. Everyone was excited for him to be re-donning his Hammer.

"Heilsa, bro," Ryland said. "I have to say, this is my first long distance Hammer-Donning. Are you ready?"

Matt answered that he was, and after consecrating the circle, they began. He remembered much of the ceremony from the first time. He pledged his loyalty to the Goðin and his kindred, and to uphold the Nine Noble Virtues. He swore to be a protector of Family, Faith, and Folk. But just when he thought that the ceremony was over, and he could put his Hammer on, Ryland had something else to say.

"Matt, I have proudly watched you grow in this way of life. Recently you stumbled and had to set your Hammer aside as you tried to find your way. None of us are perfect, but you did everything you could to once again be worthy to wear Mjöllnir. That being said, if you have to set your Hammer aside again, it will be forever. Do you understand?"

"Yes, I understand."

"Then don your Hammer now with the blessing of the Folk."

Matt looped the chain around his neck and felt overcome with emotion. It was only a piece of metal, but it was also so much more than that. He barely heard a word as Ryland passed the phone around so everyone could congratulate him. All he could think about was how far he'd come since that night in the motel room. *I did it*, he thought. *I regained my honor.*

But the small voice told him he wasn't done yet. There was still one thing he had left to do....

The Path Of Loyalty

"No one hungers as long as one comrade still possesses a piece of bread.
No one thirsts as long as one comrade still has a gulp of water.
No one is left alone as long as one comrade is still alive."
                                                            Kurt Eggers

Now that you have overcome your addiction and your Hammer is once again hanging around your neck, I will let you in on a secret:

We are at war.

The look of disbelief on your face tells me you're not convinced. That's exactly what our enemies want; for us to be uncertain of whether we're even supposed to be fighting back. It's much easier to win a war if your enemy doesn't know he's in one.

I was once like you. I believed that addiction is a weakness of our Folk, not an underhanded tactic being used against us. The truth is, it's both. I understand your uncertainty and accept it. You've been told a lie for so long, and so convincingly, that you've forgotten the truth ever existed. Its my duty to lay out the truth as logically as I can. When I'm finished, if I've done my job, you can react in one of three different ways:

You can believe me and refuse to fight back, in which case you're a coward.

You can believe me and throw in with our enemies for gain, in which case you're a traitor.

Or you can believe me and fight back, in which case I'm proud to call you my brother.

The Opium Wars

How tactically brilliant would it be to fight a war where you use your enemies' weakness against him? Kill him or destroy his will without firing a single shot? Erode public support so that his own people don't even **want** him to win the war?

That's exactly what our European ancestors did to the Chinese in the mid-1800s. In an attempt to halt white expansion, the Chinese enacted many restrictions on European merchants. Predictably, this only led to a thriving black market, where Europeans, seeing that the Chinese had a taste for opium, began trading drugs for goods. Opium addiction rates skyrocketed even as the Chinese government did everything they could to combat the flow of drugs. When China placed an embargo on Britain, Britain retaliated by sending a military force into Hong Kong and Chiankiang. China was no match for the British army and when the war was over, the Chinese were forced to make many concessions. The Chinese government tried to rebel one more time which led to the second Opium War and ultimately legalization of the trade in opium.

This should be an example of just how very hard it is to stem the tide of drugs into a country. And keep in mind, the Chinese government did everything in their power to **stop** the opium from coming in.

This wasn't the first time such tactics were considered. In the first century AD the historian Tacitus studied the Germanic tribes. He wrote, "For their drink, they draw a liquor from barley or other grain; and ferment the same so as to make it resemble wine... In extinguishing thirst they use not equal temperance. If you will but humor their excess in drinking, and supply them with as much as they covet, it will be no less easy to vanquish them by vices than by arms."

The man Kurt Eggers who was quoted at the top of this chapter would say something very similar almost 2000 years later. "Whoever wants to strengthen the German, must force him to distress and deprivation. That is the secret of German nature: The German soul has never yet been endangered in wars, but often in cowardly times of peace. In prosperous times the German is unsuspecting and happy like a child. It is easy for his enemies to tame him with theories and strange doctrines. Then they can dare to exploit him and force him to debasing slave tasks."

Today's War

It makes sense that if these tactics were used in the past, they could be used in the present. Follow the profits from that gram of dope up the chain and you're likely to find an enemy of our Folk. It could be a cartel flooding our borders with narcotics or Muslim extremists cultivating opium for sale in the U. S. and Europe. Do you really think they're putting the profits in a college fund so their children can get out of the drug trade? Hell no. They're funneling those profits into more land, crops and vehicles to more effectively pump poison into our children's veins.

And don't think for a second its only foreigners who are profiting off us. The pharmaceutical industry, those privateers of pain meds, are preying on our weakness. Here's a statistic that illuminates the vicious cycle they're creating. West Virginia, arguably the state hardest hit by the opioid epidemic, has a population of 1.8 million. One drug manufacturer has sent a shipment of enough pills for every person to receive 430 doses per year. In Huntington, WV, every four times a fire truck leaves the station, at least one will be for an overdose. Over 2000 overdoses are expected in 2017.

And don't look for the government to help. They have a history of turning a blind eye when security, profits, or votes are involved. Who knows which Islamic puppet group they're training to be the next Al-Qaeda or which prescription drug company is donating millions to the Superpacs. And as for the cartels to the south of us, get used to them. With the changing demographics in the country, politicians are well aware that their careers depend on the Hispanic vote.

Throughout this book I've tried to steer clear of any political or racial issues. In our Hofguild, one of the rules we follow is to leave those issues at the door. There is already a big enough divide between Ásatrúar in the free world and Ásatrúar in prison. Many Ásatrúar in the free world (who I hear have begun calling themselves Norse Pagans) view those in prison as a bunch of Neo-Nazi haters. And conversely, Ásatrúar in prison view those in the free world as fluffy bunny liberals. This stubborn individualist mindset and inability to come together is simultaneously our greatest strength and greatest weakness.

Regardless of where you fall on the issue of whether De'kwan should be allowed in the kindred, I think we can all agree on one thing: The majority of people drawn to Asatru are of European descent. Therefore, the greatest impact we can have is in cleaning up our own communities.

You see this all the time in prison, which is a microcosm of our society. There is a diversity of groups: Bloods, Crips, G. D.'s, Aryans, Hispanics, Muslims, Five Percenters, NOI, Moorish Science, DMI, Christians, Wiccans, and Jews. While we coexist peacefully (most of the time) there is a sharp divide. As the head of the Asatru group, I can't go tell a Muslim what to do. Even if I was doing it with good intentions, that love-your-neighbor, universal brotherhood shit doesn't work in here. Doesn't work too well in the real world, either, from what I can see. If I want to see effective change, I have to make sure my guys are moving the right way. I have to lead by example and align myself with like-minded, noble individuals in other communities. (Because it never fails that one or two people hold the influence in any group.) I have to clean up my doorstep and not worry about the next man's. In fact, the only time I worry about the next man is when he oversteps his bounds.

All I'm trying to say is we need to worry less about the Utgard, and more about changing ourselves for the better.

How do we fix our communities? I wish I could say there's an easy, one-size-fits-all solution to the drug problem, but I've come this far without lying to you and I'm not going to start now. We will have to attack the problem from many angles and many different levels in order to win this war.

Here are some possible solutions as I see them.

We have to understand human nature and group dynamics when structuring our kindreds. The direction of any kindred will be determined by the majority, or by those with the strongest personalities. If the majority view hard drug use as okay, then that sets the tone for new members. But if a critical mass feel that hard drug use is counter to our way of life, it changes the tone. Peer pressure works both ways.

We have to raise our children the correct way. This means teaching them to be proud of their heritage and respect diversity while not falling victim to the propaganda of guilt. Children who are brainwashed into feeling ashamed of who they are may resort to drugs to bolster their self-esteem.

Education is key. Instead of using scare tactics that can backfire in the end, every parent should honestly discuss the dangers of drug use with their children.

Instead of simply warehousing people, prison needs to offer rehabilitation. Right now, rehabilitation is a joke. I've been locked up for ten years and haven't completed a single program, despite trying. Sixteen years from now, right before I go home, DOC will push me through a reentry program. Everything I've done to learn and better myself has been self-motivated. Oh, and drugs are as easy to get in prison as they are on the street. All you taxpayers are footing the bill for junkies to lay around and get high all day. It's Welfare with razor wire.

Drug companies who push out amounts of pills in excess of any reasonable demand should be held accountable. They should have to pay fines the same way Big Tobacco did. These fines should be used for treatment.

On the Path of Loyalty, your task is to do everything in your power to help those who still struggle with addiction. As one who knows firsthand the pitfalls of recovery, you are better suited for this task than anyone. Become a sponsor and use this program to make a difference.

Wassail.

Matt's Saga

Matt pulled up to a rundown trailer out in County View and killed his lights. He'd been here before and knew he would have to move quick. He shoved the pipe in his waistband and stepped into the rain.

As he made his way through mounds of trash bags and beer cartons, he noticed the curtains twitch. Shit. He'd already been spotted. It was impossible to sneak up on a crackhead.

He banged on the front door three times before a pissed off voice called out he was coming. Matt recognized the voice of Twitch, a crackhead who slung just enough to get high. There was a pause as Twitch looked through the peephole and said, "Go away, Matt. I don't want no trouble."

"Me neither. Just let me in."

"There's no reason for you to be here. I heard you put down the pipe."

"I don't know who you heard that from. I've got my pipe on me right now."

Twitch didn't reply for a long moment like he was considering opening the door. Maybe this would go the easy way.

No such luck. Twitch said, "If you don't leave I'm callin the cops."

"Yeah? I fucking doubt it." Matt took a half step back and front kicked the door, right by the handle. The flimsy wood exploded inward. He heard a thud and muffled cursing as he barreled his way inside.

He quickly scanned his surroundings. He was in a living room/dining room which was partitioned into smaller sections with comforters hanging from the ceiling. It reminded him of the sheet forts he used to make as a kid. Beside him, Twitch was bent over, clutching his face, blood streaming through his splayed fingers. He wasn't a threat so Matt ignored him and started to search the trailer.

I can't believe I used to live like this, Matt thought, as he surveyed the filth around him. Every time he pulled a blanket back, hungry eyes stared back at him, sizing him up to see if he might have a hit.

Moving into a long hallway, he started snatching doors open. The third door he opened revealed a large man in bed with a woman. He saw the blond hair and his stomach knotted. But then the woman rolled over and he saw she was in her forties. He breathed a sigh of relief.

"Hey asshole, who told you to come in here?" the man asked. He climbed out of bed, tugging up a pair of basketball shorts. Matt pulled the pipe from his waistband, hiding it behind his thigh. When the man tried to grab him, Matt swung the pipe. There was a sharp crack and suddenly the man was on the ground cradling his broken wrist. Matt continued his search down the hall.

He found Aaryn in the last room on the right. She was curled up on a dirty futon. She looked terrible. Her typically tan skin was waxy and pale except for the black bags beneath her eyes. She was clutching one of the crack pipes shaped like a glass rose that they sold in gas stations. He took it from her and crushed it beneath his boot. The noise woke her. She blinked in confusion. "Matt? Is that you?"

"It's me."

"What are you doing here?"

"I came to get you out of here. You're better than this."

Aaryn self-consciously tried to fix her hair before bursting into tears. "Better than what? You don't know me at all anymore. You don't know the things I've done".

"Forget all that. It doesn't matter. All that matters is me and you are walking out that door and never looking back."

"You left me. And now you make it sound like we're just going to live happily ever after? Like it's that easy." Just as suddenly as they started, Aaryn's tears dried up. She balled her fists up and started hitting Matt on the chest. "I hate you! Just go away."

Matt grabbed her wrists, wincing when he felt how thin they were. He wrapped her in a tight embrace, whispering in her ear as she struggled. "I'm not leaving. You stuck by me through everything and I'm going to show you the same loyalty. So either you get in my truck, or I'm going to sit here until the cops come and arrest me for malicious wounding."

Matt couldn't tell if his words were having any effect. But at least she'd stopped struggling so he kept talking.

"But if you come with me, we'll make the life we always planned to. I'm not saying it will be easy. It will be the hardest thing you've ever had to do. But you know what else? It'll be worth it. I promise you. Now will you please just come with me?"

Aaryn didn't say anything for a long time. He almost didn't hear her when she finally whispered, "I missed you so much."

"I missed you, too."

By the time they climbed in the truck, Matt could hear sirens wailing in the distance. They were too far away. After a few stressful minutes he was on the interstate, heading towards the Oceanfront. He'd rented a room at the Turtle Cay, a four star resort, for a week. At least Aaryn would be comfortable as she kicked.

Matt snuck a glance at Aaryn in the passenger seat. She looked so frail and scared, but just for a moment he saw her as she used to be, and how he knew she could be again. He would do whatever he could to help her.

Fehu (fay-hoo)

Symbolizes: Gold ~ Cattle ~ Mobile Wealth ~ Fertility ~ Energy

---

At first glance, the meaning of this rune doesn't seem to have much significance in modern life. Let's face it, the only time most of us come across cattle is when it comes with fries and a Coke. Yet to our ancestors, cattle, goats and sheep were considered to be signs of wealth, prestige, and security. During plentiful times they could be milked or bred and during hard times they could be butchered or sold. Cattle was a currency that was accepted everywhere.

Our currency has evolved to cash, credit cards and Paypal. Still, when you break these into their most elemental form, they're all simply a transmission of energy. If I want something and find enough pieces of inherently worthless pieces of paper, then like magic, it can be mine. When applied correctly, the concept of mobile wealth keeps a society running smoothly.

But if fehu is abused, the outcome is disastrous. The negative aspects of fehu are greed, usury, exploitation, and the breakdown of higher values. This is exhibited in the man who uses his money, assets, or talents for negative purposes. Those who are consumed by fehu are rarely able to transcend spiritually and often die straw deaths.

It's easy to see how this rune applies to the drug industry since it's a lifestyle which is founded on exploitation. Those who are the most ruthless, the most blind to the pain around them, rise to the top. Just imagine how much energy an ounce of meth can mobilize. Over there some stickup kids kicked in a dealer's door and shot his kid on accident. And here's a young girl with nothing to sell but herself, turning tricks for any john with a twenty rock. All this money gets funneled up the chain. It really doesn't matter who's at the top; they're an enemy of our Family, Faith, and Folk.

The drugs themselves are neither good or evil. They simply mobilize energy in the form of chemical reactions. Most of these

81

chemicals already exist in our bodies, but are amplified or blocked from draining off as normal.

Fehu is a helpful rune to meditate on during recovery as the positive energies are reasserting themselves in unfamiliar channels. Exercise, rest, and nutritious foods will help the process. Another viewpoint is that you will have more money to spend now that you're no longer blowing it on drugs. Reward yourself with something that you've wanted but could never afford. When you're ready to take the next step, combine fehu with the principles of ingwaz and invest in your future.

I could go on and on about how fehu relates to different aspects of addiction, but I'll leave you with a simple image. Go look at a cow with its dull, glassy eyes and its stupid, contented expression. Now go look at a junkie. Any questions?

Uruz (oo-ruse)

Symbolizes: Aurochs ~ Primal Strength ~ Vitality ~ Organic Transformation

---

An outpouring of energy that cannot be contained by will alone; a breaking forth from safe and secure channels with an abundance of life affirming vitality; this is uruz.

The word uruz derives from aurochs, an extinct form of European bison known for its size and strength. There were varying degrees of holiness among cattle, ranging from the common milk cow to the blóted animal. According to Gronbech, the sacrificial animal was always chosen for its size and beauty and its consecration expanded this power even more.

What this means is our ancestors not only recognized strength as a virtue, they considered it holy, a manifestation of the divine. No timid hearts beat in their chests. They did not glorify meekness and false humility. Great men and women were not pulled down from the heights by squinty-souled thralls. Life was a celebration. One of the two humans who will survive Ragnarok is Lifthrasir "Yearning for Life".

Do you yearn for life, or do you endure it?

The negative aspects of uruz are repression, weakness, and denial of power. These mindsets are plaguing our Folk. But it wasn't always like this. At one time we were discoverers, conquerors, creators of civilization. Now we have been made to regret our history and watch monuments of our heroes be torn down. Guilt and apathy have placed fetters on our pride and our hope for the future.

One of the reasons that drugs are so alluring is because they release these pent-up forces. Methamphetamine releases our unconscious uruz. Meth addicts often describe a rush of euphoria, sharper sights, more vivid sounds. They feel more energetic and self-confident. When the drug wears off the world seems dull by comparison.

The saddest part is, this feeling of confidence could be our natural state. Since it's not, we should examine the underlying problem; our lack of purpose. Nietzsche said it best; a man with a strong enough *why* can bear any *how*. This means we can shoulder any burden if our life is fulfilling. Instead we deny every action that makes our heart ring true as we live lives of quiet desperation. Many try to find excitement and push their limits with drugs and alcohol. We drink until we pass out. We drug until we OD. We press against the fringes of our sanity with hallucinogens just to say we've been there.

This urge to engage in risky behavior is normal. Our ancestors never felt more alive than when they risked death. But drug use is a two-edged sword; it fills that urge even as it saps your strength and vitality. There are so many better ways to test yourself. Extreme sports, mountain climbing and Crossfit to name a few. Or if you like to get drunk and fight, then cut out the middleman, join an MMA gym, and fuck somebody up. At least then you can be a role model for our Folk, not dying a straw death in some trap house with a needle in your arm.

Or, better yet, find a cause that you feel strongly about and give your life to it.

Thurisaz (thoo-ri-soz)

Symbolizes: Active Defense ~ Action ~ Destruction

Thurisaz is the rune of active defense, the will and the balance between order and chaos. Its literal meaning is thorn; fitting because the thorn is what protects the flower from being trampled or handled irreverently. The god associated with thurisaz is Thor, Thurses' Bane, who actively defends Midgard from the Jötnar.

Active defense is an important concept of natural law. It is similar to frith in that both are active pursuits of peace. In The Culture of the Teutons, Gronbech describes the difference between peace and active defense.

"Security, but with a distinct note of something active, something willing and acting, or something at least which is ever on the point of action. A word such as the Latin *pax* (peace) suggests first and foremost - if I am not in error - a laying down of arms, a state of equipoise due to the sense of disturbing elements; frith, on the other hand, indicates something armed, protection, defence - or else a power for peace which keeps men amicably inclined. Even when we find mention, in the Germanic, of "making peace", the fundamental idea is not that of removing disturbing elements and letting things settle down, but that of introducing a peace power among the disputants."

Active defense is the mindset we take towards our recovery. We don't lay down our arms and surrender, hoping that the urge to get high will go away. We fight, every day, to remain sober. Our bodies are Midgard and anything or anyone who threatens our sobriety is from Utgard.

What are some of the steps you can actively take to defend your recovery?

1. Lose your drug dealer's cell number.
2. Tell all your get-high buddies to lose yours.

85

3. Find a heathen sponsor who can bolster your commitment when it starts to falter.

4. Substitute your need to get high with a healthy alternative such as MMA, Crossfit, or weightlifting.

5. Get out of your own head and go help someone else. It doesn't have to be drug related help. There are plenty of worthy causes that you can lend a hand to. Not only will it distract you from your own problems, you're also practicing hospitality.

There's a reason that Thor was the most popular of all the Goðin. While Odin was respected, and yes, often feared, Thor was loved by the common man. He had a straightforward nature, quick to anger and quick to forget. But most importantly he was not one to sit idly by when he could help a friend or kinsmen. Our lore is filled with stories of Thor coming to the aid of others and actively defending the Folk. In Lokasenna, when Loki was slandering the Goðin, they tried to use diplomacy to get him to shut up. This only spurred Loki on. It was only after Thor arrived in the hall that Loki realized the wisdom of silence.

Take heed of this lesson from Thor. Some enemies you can't reason with, you can only fight.

Ansuz (ahn-sooz)

Symbolizes: Inspiration   ~
Divine Breath ~ Mouth of Odin

The single greatest scourge holding our people in thrall is undeniably drug addiction. In our world today we have parents neglecting their children, we have our young massed along the streets selling their bodies, and we hear of brother betraying brother all for the same reason: Their unquenchable desire for the imagined euphoric release drugs grant from a world slowly circling the toilet. Our society has devolved into a misanthropic nest of vipers surviving on the ruin of kith and kin. Oblivion is the only logical outcome for a society surviving through a constant altered state of awareness.

What can be done to alter the course of devastation and corruption humanity stumbles upon? What can I do to stem the tide of addiction threatening the lives of those I love with disillusion? Can one man make a difference in the life of another? What can you do to help bring our people back from the brink of destruction? Sadly, there is no magic pill. If there was, someone would have found a way to market it by now. There are no easy answers and the solution will vary from individual to individual.

How can ansuz impact addiction in your life? Ansuz is explained as a god, usually Odin. Ansuz is also explained as the "mouth of God". Sounds and vibrations are a powerful force throughout all existence. Everything ever accomplished was communicated through the application of sound. This is why the Christians cut out the tongues of our greatest historical leaders.

At the conclusion of the Havamol, Odin speaks of the eighteen songs he knows for all things opposing a good and prosperous life. These songs are undoubtedly a chanting of the runar and ansuz is manifest in each and every one. It is important to note that Allfather's first song deals with sickness, pain, and sorrow

"The songs I know, that King's wives know not,

Nor men that are the sons of men
The first is called hope, and help it can bring thee
In sorrow and pain and sickness"

What more is addiction than pain, sickness, and sorrow? This is Odin's suggestion, for he never commands. The power of ansuz is in tapping into the power of sound to direct our inner strength so we can gain control and overcome that which hinders us from moving toward greatness.

Most desirable things are difficult to attain. Nobody wakes up one day and discovers themselves "addicted." It is a process, addiction, that takes months, often years, and by the time awareness dawns, most of our lives are in ruins. For most, the road to recovery is a long and arduous process, but if the restoration of our lives holds any value, this process is worth the effort.

The meditative power of ansuz would be a great jumping-off point for anyone with the heart and desire to reclaim their soul and move proudly toward that which is becoming. Sadly, most people view meditation and chanting as foreign concepts. Nothing could be farther from the truth. Singing, laughter, and words of kindness are all forms of chanting. Every time you embrace another you enter into a shared meditative state, though it lasts for but a moment. Positive words of hope and encouragement are all chants aimed at moving the recipient toward goodness and fulfillment.

In the quietest hour of your day, sit and focus on a hope or dream. Think of a loved one and your desire to share a prosperous life with that individual. Picture their face. Hear their voice and feel the warmth of their smile.

Relax.

Take long deep breaths.

Let the power of ansuz flow through you.

(Aaahhhnnn-suuuz)

Aaahhhnnn-suuuz.

Aaahhhnnn-suuuz.

Hold no shame. Feel the love of your ancestors as they witness you reclaiming your birthright. Let the pain flow away and embrace the possibilities of love, joy, and companionship from those who hold the best hopes for your life.

Relax.

(Aaahhhnnn-suuuz)

Aaahhhnnn-suuuz.

Aaahhhnnn-suuuz.

Turn this power toward every aspect of your life and ready yourself for the work that lies ahead.

Heil the Rune-Master!

Raido (rye ~ tho)

Symbolizes: Journey ~ Right Action ~ Ritual

Raido has a traditional meaning of journey or riding. It is symbolic of the path that lies before us all. For many of us, our drug and alcohol addictions have led us to this point in our lives: Prison. As Ásatrúar we all believe in the natural order of things and we understand that our journey has led us here. However, this is not where the path ends. It is our duty to follow the complete cycle. For me, Raido means being in charge of my own path. It means being the master of my own destiny. Whenever I meditate on this rune, the poem *Invictus* by William Henley comes to mind.

> Out of the night that covers me,
> Black as the Pit from pole to pole,
> I thank whatever Goðin may be
> For my unconquerable soul.
> In the fell clutch of circumstance
> I have not winced or cried aloud.
> Under the bludgeoning of chance
> My head is bloody, but unbowed.
> Beyond this place of wrath and tears
> Looms but the horror of the shade,
> And yet the menace of the years
> Finds, and shall find me, unafraid.
> It matters not how strait the gate,
> How charged with punishments the scroll,
> I am the master of my fate;
> I am the captain of my soul.

There is also much significance in the stave shapes that make up the raido rune. These staves are isa, wunjo, kenaz, and laguz, and together they speak the true meaning of this rune. Isa is the backbone of all runes, holding them together with unwavering strength and integrity. Wunjo is positive direction in your life, the harmony that exists in your core. Even if you are a drug abuser, there is somewhere deep inside of you that is eternal and untouched by the chaos of your surroundings. Laguz is the water of life. Water was as integral to our ancestor's survival as it is to ours. It gives us food, quenches our thirst, and transports us. Combined with the other runes it shows how our life force has sustained us on our journey. And lastly there's kenaz, the torch of intelligence and experience. This is your testimonial of everything you have learned up until this point in your life. You can use it in a positive way to help others learn from your mistakes, because in the end, we are not on a lonely trek through life. The world is filled with people we can share raido with, people we can help when they stumble, and receive help from in return.

Make the conscious decision to strive towards excellence. Let your path take you ever upward. Transcendancy is our core belief, yet by abusing drugs and alcohol we enslave ourselves to a life of stagnation. Take up your raido and break the fettered bonds. Be the master of your wyrd.

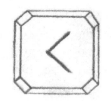

Kenaz (ke-noz)

Symbolizes: Torch ~ Creativity ~ Intelligence

Kenaz is the rune of knowledge in all its forms. It's the advice of a trusted elder, the dusty manuscript from a distant age, the hard-knock lessons we can only learn from painful experience. It is a burning need to know and understand the world around us. Used properly, it can transform us, turning intellectual knowledge into wisdom. Used haphazardly, we only acquire facts that we give no thought to.

This book is a manifestation of kenaz. The Seeds of Oak Hofguild wanted to pass the torch of our combined wisdom and experience. If we are successful in conveying our message and you are receptive then the light of kenaz is kindled between us. It is a give and take relationship.

But we often take for granted how blessed we are when it comes to knowledge. We live in a time of information overload. The answer to any question we can imagine is at our fingertips. It wasn't that long ago that only the highest class of people could read and afford books. The libraries of today that are being closed for lack of use would have been valuable beyong belief. Familiarity breeds contempt.

Yet there are even worse ways in which knowledge can be abused. One is misinformation. So many people out there tailor the truth to fit their agenda. We are assaulted by so many lies and false information that we cannot recognize the truth.

I remember when I was a kid, having a family dinner where my family discussed my DARE class. For those who are unaware, DARE stands for Drug Awareness Resistance Education. It was mandatory for middle-schoolers. That night I asked my dad about the effects of pot. "It will make you go insane," he told me. "How addictive is it?" I asked. "You'll be hooked the first time you try it." This scared the hell out of me so that I didn't experiment with pot until my sophomore year of high school. But when I finally did try it, I saw that his scare tactics were bullshit. The only insane thing about pot was how good leftover Chinese food tasted after I smoked it. These lies hurt me more in the long run because it made me think, if he was exaggerating the seriousness smoking pot, maybe he was exaggerating about the harder drugs, too.

As a teacher it is important that what we teach is the truth. Once you lose the trust of your child, your student, hell, of anyone, it is hard to get back.

Then there are the lessons I wish I never sought to learn. We've all heard that knowledge is power, but power corrupts. Years of my life were spent studying the esotericism of drug culture. I trolled Erowid message boards on how to make hash and meth. I found crackhead proffesors to teach me the best way to cut and rerock coke. I knew more about drug law and due process than most lawyers and cops. And for what? Nothing. If I could go back and tell my younger self one thing it would be: Just because you can learn anything doesn't mean you should.

Gebo (ge-bo)

Symbolizes: Gift ~ Hospitality ~
Magical Force

The meaning of the rune Gebo can be summed up in the saying, a gift for a gift. It is a rune of exchange, loyalty, altruism, and reciprocality.

When working with gebo it's important to understand that there's no such thing as getting something for nothing. There's no free lunch. In the Havamal, Odin says "better not to give than to offer too much, **a gift always seeks a return.**" When a gift is given to you by someone you love, their payoff is often the joy of seeing you happy. But gifts can be given from more sinister motives as well. Some people give to get, sacrificing some small gift or favor to get you in their pocket. Make no mistake, any gift has an invisible obligation that comes with it.

The concept of Gebo is likely ingrained in a more primitive part of our brain. It's a part of Natural Law called reciprocal altruism, which can be observed in chimpanzees. In the wild, chimps must roam far and wide in search of the fruit which is a main staple of their diets. They travel in small packs of males until they come across such a tree. You would think that the pack would hoard their find and eat off it themselves. You would be wrong. They drum their feet on the tree and whoop to call other chimps to the feast. They do it because they instinctively know that, while they were fortunate enough to find the tree this time, they may not be so lucky next time and it never hurts to have the goodwill of others.

Reciprocal altruism is also a part of the addict mentality believe it or not. I saw it all the time when I was selling coke. No sooner would I re-up and serve one person, than my phone would start blowing up. It didn't matter if I told that first customer I only had a little bit left, or I was going to sleep, he was going to spread the word. It's almost like addicts have an unspoken agreement to tell each other when a dealer gets on. It goes back to buying goodwill for those times when he's not in the know.

When we understand Gebo, we understand that anything we put out into the world, or our own spirituality, will return to us in some shape or form. This doesn't necessarily have to be an equal exchange, for Odin states in the Havamal, "Something great is not always to be given, often little will purchase praise; with half a loaf of bread and a half-drained cup I got myself a friend." As addicts, we give our vitality, our ambition, and our self-respect for a few fleeting moments of bliss and escapism. Not a fair exchange if you ask me.

We live in a world increasingly concerned with the bottom line. So what is it? What is worth sacrificing to get a better gift in return?

We need look no further than Odin. What did he value above all else?

Wisdom.

He sacrificed his eye to see more clearly. We don't have to go that far. We just have to give up those negative things that fog up our vision: shame, guilt, apathy, anger, pride, and yes, drugs. Only then will we be able to move forward on the Odinnic Path. Only then will we be worthy of the gift of wisdom.

Wunjo (woon-yo)

Symbolizes: Harmony ~ Binding ~ Frith

Imagine for a moment the most perfect day possible, the type of day you wouldn't mind living for the rest of eternity. Could you actually live in eternal decadence, chasing the same high, gorging on expensive food, reveling in mindless entertainment? Or is it possible that this would this become a torture worse than death?

For me the perfect day is much different. It's a day in which I find challenge and harmony in equal measure. My workout is harder than it's ever been yet my muscles rise to the challenge. During the interactions with my brothers we engage in conversations of substance and exist in frith even if our opinions differ. Whatever project I'm working on at the time pushes my intelligence to its limits, resulting in a finished product that is beyond my wildest expectations. The mindset of an Odinist is of someone who constantly seeks the challenge of high achievement and the joy of accomplishment. The Odinist also understands that, while change is born in the crucible of challenge, it takes harmony of body, mind, and spirit to rise to the challenge.

The Rede of Honor encapsulates the concept of wunjo where it states, "One advances individually and collectively only by living in harmony with the natural order of the world." Harmony is defined as a balanced interrelationship or internal calm. This, however, is a subjective state. The truth is, like health, harmony is something we usually only notice once it's lost. It's easier to define harmony through its opposites; chaos, conflict, and discord.

Hard drug use is one of the quickest ways to upset the harmony of the individual and the community.

As far as the individual is concerned, we'll define harmony as a balanced relationship between body, mind, and spirit. Hard drug use will upset this delicate balance in even the strongest-willed person.

Addiction usually leads to poor nutrition and lack of exercise that ruins your physique. Then there's the anxiety, unbalanced sleep, and destroyed brain cells which wreck your mind. And last, the nids and broken promises kill your spirit.

It's no different with the community. Since each individual is a part of the community, the destruction simply happens on a wider scale. Frith is broken when addicts argue over drug debts or feel like someone whom they "looked out for" by getting them high didn't return the favor. Female addicts flock to the men who can get them high, leading to further rifts and violence. Diseases spread more quickly due to a lack of inhibition and precaution. An oppressive mood of shame and distrust permeates the community that has given into addiction.

As Ásatrúar we are creating our faith every day. With every hofguild and every kindred that is born, we are literally defining what it means to be an Ásatrúar. Every choice, every concession, has an impact on the whole. That's why we must cultivate a standard of wunjo within our communities. It begins with choosing leaders who have achieved harmony in their personal lives. Because as Nyhellenia wisely said, "The sparrow follows the sower, the people their good princes." A wise leader will always focus on nurturing wunjo with his people.

So often we make life too complicated. True harmony is simple. It can be summed up in the words, "Do right and fear nothing."

Hagalaz (ha-ga-loz)

Symbolizes: Hail ~ Destruction ~ Evolution

The journey of the runar encompasses every aspect of the life our ancestors had to endure. From beginning to end we see the forces contained within the natural law. Everything that our Folk could expect to encounter was represented within the twenty-four characters of the runes.

Late spring to mid-summer was a time of emotional turmoil within the clans of the North. Great hope for the coming harvests and tremendous dread of the storms that could spell disaster for the farmer's livelihood vied for dominance in the Northman's soul. One single tempest could spell doom for not only the farmer's family, but for the people of an entire region.

Hagalaz encapsulates the hopes and concerns of our people from yesterday, and tugs at us even today. Hail, the bane of all those who live off of the land. This dreaded weather anomaly filled every farmer's heart with concern, and when this stony plague fell from the heavens, often led to great sorrow. This was the single greatest concern of our Folk.

Today, with advanced technology and super-expanded farming techniques, the failure of a single crop is no more than an inconvenience. People only fear the hailstone for whatever damage it might inflict on their pretty little toys. Every modern newscast of hailstones is invariably accompanied by photographs of shattered windshields. Not exactly the life-altering circumstances our ancestors had to contend with.

What are the hailstones of today? If the runar were revealed to us now, what would represent the Hagalaz rune? What dread, what powerful negative influence would fill the psyche of this modern generation with concern? The answer is simple. Read every "Heathen Spotlight" in our biannual publication. When asked what single thing holds our people back from attaining the greatness of their destiny, the answer has been a unanimous "drug addiction."

The modern-day hagalaz would best be represented by the crack-pipe, the needle and spoon, or the toothpaste cap. So often I have heard heathens proudly proclaim that we don't "bow" to any Goðin. But far too often otherwise good men and women bow to a synthetic god introduced by people who are alien to our culture.

Thankfully, I was not cursed by an addictive personality, and I never fell prey to the "victimized' mentality of those who were told that their own failures, shortcomings, and addictions were not their fault, that addiction is a disease.

The question begs to be asked: How do we break the grip that drug addiction holds on our people? If it was a physical addiction, and we were on a farm, I would chain you to a tree for a couple of weeks. But in this environment, in a world that lies and proclaims that "it's not your fault," I honestly don't know. In this world the lunatics are running the insane asylum, and business is good.

"Break the cycle." Cool slogan, and it sounds so easy. But to break anything is a violent, intrusive process that takes desire and an unflagging will to put down what you have picked up. If the individual doesn't truly have a desire to rid themselves of this modern-day hagalaz, then they are doomed to failure. They will never reap the bountiful harvest, and all the promise of a sparkling destiny will whither on the vine.

That which is becoming looks bleak. Our world is in disarray and our people are stumbling around with no idea of the direction they are heading. Our women are unsure with our hands on the tiller of life, but what else could we expect? Our children are lost and alone, drifting through life with nobody there to guide them, and who is to blame?

Look in the mirror if you wish to witness the devastating effects of our modern-day hagalaz. The storm is upon us. What will you do?

Naudiz (now-theez)

Symbolizes: Need-Fire ~ Friction ~ Resistance ~ Overcoming

As Ásatrúar we should always try to view the world around us honestly, without prejudgement or superstition. An important part of working with the runes is being able to open yourself to a higher knowledge and understanding, letting go of limiting preconceptions.

We search for truth even when it may be a hard truth. What I'm about to say may not be popular, especially in a book on drug recovery; however, many years of experience have shown me that those who have struggled or are struggling with addiction are stronger in many ways than those who haven't.

Since becoming goði of the Seeds of Oak, the last two brothers I've placed in the Logmaðr position are similar in many ways. Both have been doing life in installments for crimes stemming from drugs, and both openly struggle with addiction. At face value my choice for them as Logmaðr may seem unwise, considering the Logmaðr's position is about upholding the laws of the community. But the Logmaðr has the added responsibility of having to keep order, both within and outside the hall. And for that purpose they're great.

Why? I believe it comes down to the principle of naudiz.

Naudiz is a rune of overcoming adversity. Life will throw many obstacles in your path. Naudiz is about using the friction of these experiences to kindle the fire of your transformation. It is about persevering and struggling against all odds. Its about understanding that unforeseen problems may cause anxiety and that's okay. But, each problem and conflict that you survive leaves you more capable for the next.

Any leader who does not willingly embrace and seek out naudiz stands on shaky ground. Our ancestors understood this fact in a way that we have forgotten. Kings were not kings by blood or popularity. They were forged in the crucible of war because only a man capable to withstand conflict can bring peace.

The same standard of experience existed in domestic life. When a man asked for a woman's hand in marriage, the first questions her father would ask was, "Where have you been? What have you seen?" Times were harder and more dangerous back then. A father wouldn't want to hand his beloved daughter over to a man who didn't possess the courage or experience to protect her.

Our ancestors knew that naudiz was unavoidable so they consciously made it a part of their daily lives.

Today's society stands in stark contrast to their healthy attitude towards naudiz. These days children are sheltered from any type of conflict that would hurt their self-esteem. They have soccer games with no scoreboards and anti-bullying campaigns. While these ideas may be well-intended, they are ineffective. Self esteem comes from overcoming adversity, not avoiding it.

Which brings me back to my Logmaðrs, Stacy and Lucky. They have their faults, just like we all do. But when conflict arises there's no one else I'd rather have by my side. And it's all because of naudiz, the forging of the will through life experience. When a situation requires Stacy to politic with some gang leader on the yard, he's ready for it. Why? Because he's copped or sold drugs in almost every major city and dealt with many types of people. Naudiz. Or when Lucky has to get to the bottom of a dispute between group members, he has the combined experience of 20 years in prison. He's also done his fair share of conning people so he can see through other's bullshit. Naudiz.

Now, let me be clear; I'm not suggesting that young Ásatrúar should go on some junkie pilgrimage to gain life experience. I think that Stacy and Lucky would both be the first to admit that the price of their life experience through drug addiction was way too high. But I am suggesting two things. One, that we don't turn our backs on someone just because they struggle with addiction. If they can overcome the worst of their dependency, these brothers often turn out to be a major asset to our faith. And two, we need to encourage the younger generation to take risks, to embrace conflict and challenge, and to know the joy of living life dangerously without drugs.

Isa (ee-suh)

Symbolizes: Ice ~ Ego ~ Stillness

In the Havamal, Odin mentions ice as something that shouldn't be trusted until it is crossed. Isa is the rune of ice and it likewise has an untrustworthy reputation. It brings up images of Jötunheim and the chaotic Jötnar who dwell there. Images of gloomy winter days and deadly nights when our ancestors huddled by the fire just to stay alive. Many people who pull this rune focus only on its destructive nature. But no rune, including isa, is one-dimensional. Each can be positive or negative depending on the reading's context.

The reason ice is so dangerous is because you have to set foot on it before knowing whether it will hold you. Stepping onto a frozen lake is an act of blind faith. It's the same with hard drugs. I remember the first time I tried coke, wondering if it was as addictive as I'd heard. Would my willpower be strong enough to resist the chemical? Snorting the first line was like stepping foot on that icy lake. I made it halfway across before crashing through the ice and nearly drowning.

Isa can also symbolize the ego. As addicts we know all about ego and self-centeredness. No matter how much our loved ones plead for us to stop using, their words cannot penetrate our frozen shell. We are resistant to any type of change. Months and years may go by in which we do not change at all. Sure, we may seem to be constantly moving, partying, and acting out one drama or another. But the substance of our lives, the core of who we are, is in a state of arrested development.

We are drawn to the numbness that drugs bring. That euphoric feeling blots out all the pain that we don't want to feel. It is a numbness that we feel *we* control unlike the numbness of boredom, disappointment, and heartache. We never seem to remember that, when the numbness fades, those emotions still remain.

But isa also has a positive side. It can represent the gathering and storing of energy. In nature, stillness often precedes an explosion. Think of a snake pausing before it strikes. Or think of a tree during a cold snap; the forest, still and silent, before the tree explodes in a spray of splintered wood. There is a necessary duality between stillness and motion. You can't have one without the other.

We need to embrace this aspect of isa when it comes to drug recovery. Sometimes it's better to be still than to do too much, to make no decision, rather than the wrong one. This is especially true when we first get clean. Our initial reaction to this new feeling may be to do too much. We may want to go on a diet, start a new relationship, or make some other drastic change when the best thing for us may be to chill, to stop and conserve our energy.

So the next time you're stessed out, meditate on isa and absorb its stillness.

Jera (yare-uh)

Symbolizes: Harvest ~ Year ~ Cycle ~ Eternal Return

Birth, life, death, rebirth... Our existence is a cycle made up of many smaller concentric cycles. From the yearly cycle of spring, summer, fall and winter, to the monthly cycle of the moon, to the daily cycle of sunrise and sunset and everything in between. The same blood that cycled through your ancestors veins, cycles through your own. As you read this, the rise and fall of your chest is a sign of the air cycling through your lungs.

Jera is the rune of cyclical motion. Try to turn it upside down and you'll quickly see it's impossible. Like the sunwheel, jera maintains an effortless balance and poise.

This is not the case with us addicts. The cycles we create are chaotic and often deadly. There's a reason they're called vicious cycles. I can hazily remember years of my life where I was stuck in a shitty loop of re-up, get high, hustle, and crash. A loop that started with the first line of coke and ended days later with the Xanax I'd need to fall asleep. I'm not a functional addict, (whatever the hell that means) and I was never able to hold down a job or finish college. The cycle of addiction **I'd started** elbowed out any other way to live.

And the funny thing is, I actually looked down on those who lived the straightedge life, with their 9-5 jobs and normal sleep patterns. With their pay checks and paid vacation, and their incomprehensible concern over things like birthdays, holidays, and anniversaries. In a way I always will. Yet now that the people I grew up with are moving into a cycle of their lives that contains success and children, and the cycle of my life contains count times and quarterly shakedowns, I have to wonder, who's having the last laugh?

We must always remember that our orlog creates these cycles, and the difference between the self aware and the impulsive man is the difference between acting and being acted upon. The Asa-man is a

104

creator. He realizes that orlogthaedir are woven whether he wills it or not, so he chooses to walk deftly along the web of wyrd rather than flounder upon it.

Now that I've broken the cycle of addiction, I feel like I'm truly alive for the first time. I feel like my existence has meaning and welcome the challenge that every day brings. Despite being locked up, I look forward to the small cycles that make up my life. Every day I look forward to my workouts and my study time, to meals with my brothers and the quiet moments of meditation before I go to bed. Every week I look forward to our Hall where I get to see brothers who I don't get to see every day, while teaching and learning about our way of life. Then on Sundays I get to call my family who are now proud of the man I've become. Every year I look forward to softball season, to the High Holy Days, and to accomplishing whatever goals I've set. When the cycle of this sentence comes to an end, I look forward to the beginning of a new cycle of freedom.

Until Ragnarok, Hati and Skoll chase the sun and moon. The wolves hunger is all consuming, like that first hit which sets you off and running. But like the wolves who will never catch their prey until everything is destroyed, you will never fill that insatiable hunger by feeding it. You will chase it and chase it until it utterly consumes you.

Eiwaz (ai-voz)

Symbolizes: Vertical Cosmic Axis ~ Life/Death ~ Yew Tree

Of all the trees sacred to our ancestors, the yew tree is the most sacred. It was said that this tree broke all three planes of existence. Its roots dwelled in Helheim, its trunk in Midgard, and its branches reached into Asgard.

When on the topic of drug addiction, I take this rune as if the tree represents myself. We are sacred beings brought forth by Odin, Hoenir, and Lodurr. In our normal state we exist as the trunk, interacting with those here on Midgard. We thrive on this plane of consciousness since it is what we're most accustomed to experiencing through our five senses. Now as our consciousness fluctuates, we can move up or down the trunk into its roots or branches. This means we can change our level of interaction with the world around us by choice. Raising yourself to the top of the tree is difficult; it's done through healthy living, research, meditation, and perseverance. This is called enlightenment, transcendence, god head, etc.

By abusing drugs you move further and further down the trunk. Eventually you'll get to the point where you can no longer successfully interact with those around you. Your way of thinking fractures from the norm as you delve into the darker places of your mind. This is similar to how the roots of a tree reach into dead organic matter in the earth; things that were once whole are now broken into their basic parts to be used by higher beings. Drug addiction hurts us all. It fractures every part of our lives: relationships, work, and family.

Many of you are probably thinking that there are many cultures who use drugs for religious experiences. Hermeticism has a term called corrosive waters which means using typically harmful substances or practices to break through a mental or spiritual plateau. In the Volsung Saga, Sigmund uses corrosive waters (snake venom) to test the worth of Signy's sons. He hides a poisonous adder in a sack of flour and instructs each boy to bake him a loaf of bread. Two of the sons failed the test. Only Sinfiotli passed the initiation by kneading the adder into the flour, proving his spirit and courage. Even so, Sigmund tells Sinfiotli not to eat the bread. Unlike Sigmund who had a more purified spirit, Sinfiotli could not taste poison unharmed.

The yew tree is a good analogy for corrosive waters and drug addiction. Every part of the yew tree, save one, will kill you. The roots, the bark, and the branches are deadly, but the tree produces a berry that can be eaten. Ingesting any other part will result in death. Both life and death exist side by side in this plant. There is an extract that can be taken and used to treat cancers and one that can relieve swelling. This goes to show how drugs can help or harm us depending on how we use them.

I can see the purpose of using natural substances such as marijuana, mushrooms, or peyote to reach an altered state of consciousness. With proper dosage and guidance, they can help break through barriers and see past the mundane. But let's be real; have you ever picked up a pipe or a needle for a mystical experience?

As Ásatrúar we should always strive to be a better version of ourselves. This is something that is completely obtainable. As you move up the tree through healthy living and perseverance you will obtain a better understanding of self and the world around you.

Pertho (pur-tho)

Symbolizes: Lot Cup ~ Orlog ~ Constant Change

Whenever I used to pull this rune, I would think of dice bouncing on the floor, their numbers flashing through possibilities before settling on a single outcome. It is the essence of chance, chaos, or "what is becoming."

As addicts we have an intimate relationship with pertho. When your focus revolves around your next fix, your life becomes one big lot cup. Does this heroin dealer have a conscience, or did he cut his dope with something that will send me to my Helthing early? Does hot sink water really kill HIV and Hep C? Or, did that crackwhore really burn her lip on a pipe, or is that herpes? Step right up, and shake the lot cup, see what you get.

(The answers to the above questions are maybe, definitely not, and why risk it.)

We may not love to take risks or to live in a constant state of ambiguity, but when the only other option is to stop getting high and to live with awareness, well, we take the easy way out. We embrace chance, and call it living in the moment.

But take a minute to really think about this next question: is there really such a thing as chance? Let's look closer at the example of throwing dice. It appears to be the essence of chance. However, the orderly laws of physics such as rotation, momentum, and ricochet determine what number the die will land on. I'd be willing to bet that this isn't a gamble at all, that some scientist somewhere could devise a formula to predict the outcome as soon as the dice left your hand.

So how does this apply to real life? It demonstrates that nothing which happens to us is truly random. If you catch a disease from a dirty needle, don't blame the Norns or wyrd. The needle was infected by a long line of bad decisions, culminating in your bad decision to stick it in your arm. If some stripper ODs in your trailer, the root causes are probably drugs, lust, and daddy issues. Accept it and call 911.

I have the words "Amor Fati" tattooed on my knuckles. I tell people it means "I love fat chicks" but it really means "A love of fate." It's a philosophy that Nietzsche and Goethe discussed and lived by. It's not the idea of fate as being some foregone conclusion, written in stone before you were born. It's a mindset where you accept whatever comes your way with a strong and valiant heart. My day of death has already been decided, what I do between now and then is up to me. I love my fate because I'm not a coward. I love my fate because I'm not a shirker.

But most of all, I love my fate because it is **mine**.

There is a cause for every effect. Some causes may be obvious, others more obscure, but if you look hard enough, from the right perspective, you'll always find it. The only way we can transcend our current limitations is to start living with more awareness. Once we begin to take responsibility for our actions and their outcomes, we become co-creators of our wyrd. We walk deftly along the strands of the web, instead of floundering upon it.

Elhaz (el-hoz)

Symbolizes: Protection ~ Life ~ Elk

The first time I ever led a blot was when I understood the paradoxical nature of Elhaz. Try this: stand with your back to a room, head tilted skyward with your eyes closed, arms raised above you like a "V". How vulnerable does that feel? If you suddenly had to defend yourself from an attack, more than likely it would be too late. Not to mention your most vital areas are exposed. Yet this is the stadrgaldr for Elhaz, the rune of protection and life. How is that possible?

The answer is quite simple. When leading a blot, the room you are standing in front of isn't just any room. It's the Hall, a Ve-Stead filled with true brothers, existing in frith. If they are behind you, who can harm you? If they decide to turn on you, who can protect you? Therefore, like the heathen handshake, the elhaz stance is a sign of absolute trust amongst kinsmen.

That's why, when I pull this rune, my first thought is trust. Without trust there can be no frith. Without frith we might as well not even call ourselves a community. At that point we're just a bunch of individuals posing as something more.

I tell my brothers I can deal with anything but a liar. A thief only steals your possessions; a liar tries to steal your reality. When you lie to me you insult my intelligence, but more importantly you sow a seed of doubt that blooms in the most inopportune moments. It's hard to fully back someone who has lied to you in the past.

Once someone is knowledgeable enough about this way of life to understand how much we value our word, and they lie anyway, you can't be hard enough on them. There's only a few reasons that people lie. One is fear. The other is guilt. Both are unacceptable.

I've witnessed firsthand how hard drug use can erode the trust between friends. Back when I sold coke, my girlfriend had a bunch of friends who would drive all the way from Tappahanock to Tidewater to cop from me. The first few weekends they would all throw their money together for an ounce. The bag would sit on the coffee table all night for everyone to share. This went on for about a month. Soon after that, they would cop a half ounce, but by the end of the night they were each buying personal bags on the low. Eventually it became everyone for themselves. They would buy grams and sneak off into the bathroom to do them alone or with one other person. Arguments arose over who owed who money, or who got the others high more often. They would lie about how much coke they had left. What started off as a group of friends partying and having fun together devolved into everyone for themselves. The drugs brought to the surface the sneaky, greedy aspects of everyone's character. It took less than one summer for them all to stop being friends.

Is this what we want for our communities? As if we don't have enough problems on the outside, do we want to self-destruct from within? I don't. I want to surround myself with true brothers so I can stand in elhaz confidently, knowing that they're watching my back, not trying to stab me in it.

Sowilo (so-wih-lo)

Symbolizes: Sun ~ Life

Of all the runes in the Elder Futhark, I believe sowilo best explains the positive aspects of substance abuse recovery. This rune's traditional meaning is sun, but its otherwise known as the victory rune. After all, isn't beating a chemical dependence a major victory? I believe so.

Sowilo is associated with spiritual guidance and leadership, and with the process of individualism, or the inner self. Within substance abuse and addiction, many destructive forces are at work, and recovery often seems impossible. Being able to identify and process the many facets of Sowilo can turn this seemingly hopeless task into one more achievable. If we study our runes, and look deep within ourselves we will find that nothing is impossible unless we simply lack the desire to make it happen.

When I think of Sowilo I think of the sun. I think of new beginnings and of having a fresh chance at achieving greatness. I think of the nurturing power that the sun gives us and the destructive capabilities it also possesses. Drugs have the same set of attributes. They can heal us or harm us. It all depends on how they are used. This is how I correlate the sun aspect of substance abuse.

I think back to the days when I was using heavily and it was like the sun was my enemy. After a long night of partying it was the last thing I wanted to see coming up. Blackout curtains covered my windows. On the rare occasions I did have to go outside in the daylight, dark sunglasses covered my eyes. Beneath Sunna's loving rays I felt ashamed and exposed. It was an unnatural way to live.

I see now that we are given each day as a gift, and the sun is a constant reminder of that. If we are struggling and truly desire change, we should watch a sunrise and know that we possess the power within ourselves to do so.

As mentioned before, Sowilo is also associated with victory. It's connected to the sun in ways that nurture us and provide us with the right views and understanding needed to wage war on the battlefields of our inner selves. The victory aspect follows directly behind. When we use the power within to make positive changes in our lives, we are forever winning these battles. Having the desire to stop using drugs or alcohol is only half the war. The other half is doing it. Not many people succeed, but for the ones that do, the sun will never shine brighter and the victory will forever be honored. I can say that with absolute certainty, and from my own personal experience.

Tiwaz (tee-vaz)

Symbolizes: Justice ~ Victory ~
Self Sacrifice ~ Týr

Tiwaz, or Týr's rune, is symbolic of judgement and self-sacrifice. It is a rune of order and stability within the individual, the community, and throughout the nine worlds.

Whenever I draw this rune, I think about any decisions I might be called upon to make as a leader. I search my views for any biases or prejudices which may influence my decision in an unjust way. Tiwaz is a rune which always brings to mind the saying from the Rede of Honor, "All that you do will return to you, sooner or later, for good or for ill. Thus strive always to do good to others, or at least strive always to be just." Adherence to the concept of tiwaz is what separates a true leader from a politician.

When it comes to tiwaz and drug addiction, I correlate the two through the story of Týr and Fenris. Týr was a mighty god, renowned for his swordsmanship and his level head. He was often asked to rule on issues amongst the Goðin.

One day the Goðin gathered to express a growing concern about one of Loki's children, the Fenris wolf. They had known and loved Fenris since he was a small pup. They often made a game of feeding Fenris who had a voracious appetite and never seemed to get full. But before they knew it, Fenris had grown so big, that the Goðin knew, without some type of intervention, he would eventually consume the nine worlds.

The Goðin came to the conclusion that they would somehow have to bind the wolf. Problem was, he would never succumb to fetters voluntarily. They would have to trick him.

They approached Fenris like it was a game. "Let us see how strong you are, Fenris. A wolf as strong as you should have no trouble breaking this fetter." To their dismay he broke the first fetter *Ldingr*, and the second *Dromi*.

The situation looked grim. Fearing that nothing could restrain the massive beast, they decided to take one last shot. They sent Odr to Svartalfheim in order to commission a final fetter. The dvergar put all his skill into the magical fetter, crafting it from six impossible things: The sound of a cat's footsteps, the beard of a woman, the roots of a mountain, the sinews of a bear, the breath of a fish, and the spittle of a spider. The dvergar called this fetter Glepnir.

When the Goðin brought Glepnir to Fenris, the wolf was leery. Something told him this fetter was not like the rest, so he struck a deal. He would allow them to bind him under one condition: One of the Goðin must place their sword arm in his mouth. That way, if he could not break free and they refused to release him, he would have his wergild.

Týr immediately volunteered to place his sword hand in the wolf's mouth. It probably never seriously crossed Fenris's mind that Týr would willingly sacrifice his hand. In a warrior's society, a man's sword hand was everything. But after weighing his own personal happiness against the lives of those he loved, Týr made the sacrifice without hesitation.

I have heard interpretations that Týr, being a god, could regenerate his hand. Personally, I don't believe this to be the case. Not that Týr **couldn't** regenerate his hand, but that he **wouldn't**. His hand stood as wergild and to cheat in such a way would be breaking troth. Týr is too honorable for that. Regardless of what you believe, the point of the story is that sometimes it's necessary to make sacrifices for the good of others.

How does this story tie into drug addiction? Like many stories in our lore, it can be read in a variety of ways. Symbolically, wolves represent greed or gluttony. It's not a far stretch to correlate the wolf with the addiction centre in your brain. At first it's small and manageable, but the more you feed it, the bigger it gets until eventually you lose all control. At this point Týr, your "conscious mind", does one of two things. It keeps feeding the wolf and lets the addiction kill him/her, or it seeks to bind it. The bonds represent your self-restraint. Even bound, the addiction is always there, lurking in the background. Týr's missing hand is the part of your brain that remains damaged. You will always have a weakness to that drug. It's only your discipline and perseverance that keeps the wolf in check.

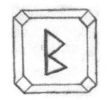

Berkano (bur-khan-o)

Symbolizes: Birch Goddess ~ Birth ~ Life Cycle

This rune at a glance seems to have little significance with addiction and recovery. Yet if you dive deeper you can correlate both aspects of berkano, the birch tree and divine powers.

First we will start with the stave shape. Three runes make up Berkano: The first is Isa, the second is wunjo, and the last is kenaz. Now, as feminine powers go, these runes are the epitome of a woman. Isa can represent the solid unwavering nature of women in our lives. This is evident to those if us who are in prison. Often our mothers, sisters, and wives stick around even when it seems the whole world has turned their backs on us. Wunjo shows both positive and negative aspects in Berkano. It symbolize the joy and harmony women can bring, as well as the chaos and harm they have the potential to inflict. And last is kenaz, which bridges the gap between harmony and chaos, showing us that no matter the result we will leave knowing more about ourselves and the world around us.

Ehwaz (eh-vaz)

Symbolizes: Horse ~ Fertility ~
Spiritual Travel ~ Partnership

Traditionally the ehwaz rune symbolizes the horse. To our ancestors, the horse was a symbol of prestige, a means of transportation, and a weapon of war. It's not hard to imagine a situation in which a quality horse could spell the difference between life and death. But times have changed. If we take "horse" as the literal definition, then this is another rune which seems to have lost its significance for modern man. Unless you live in a rural area, it's likely that horses don't play a major role in your life.

I personally believe that the runes are timeless symbols. When Odin hung on the world tree he didn't gain wisdom that would only last until the Industrial Age. When working with the runes as focal points you have to simplify them to their core meaning.

A horse represents transportation, yes, but it is more than that. In modern times we have a tendency to only look at an object for its utility, or what it can do for us. This wasn't the case with our ancestors. They took a more holistic view of the world, realizing that everything in nature has a soul. The horse, an animal they shared a close relationship with, was especially venerated. The partnership between rider and horse is about freedom.

How does ehwaz tie in to drug addiction? I equate this rune with the sponsor. The horse and the sponsor will help you carry your burden. Both will take you where you want to go.

A good horse is valuable and so is a good sponsor. When buying a horse you should check its teeth, its gait, and its spine. You don't want an old sway-backed horse. These things aren't as important when it comes to your sponsor but he still should meet certain qualifications.

What makes a good sponsor? Well first he should have a great bullshit detector; his ears should perk up at the first sign you're trying to run a con game. Ideally, he should be a recovered addict who

117

knows the lay of the land and what potholes to look out for. He should be a nag at times. He should also be someone who's available when you need him, ready to saddle up whether it's midday or midnight. But most importantly he should be someone who loves his folk and has their best interest at heart.

You can tell a lot about a man by the way he treats his sponsor. It's often a thankless job. Don't overburden him with problems you can carry yourself. He's not a pack mule. If he seems to be dejected every so often, offer **him** words of encouragement. Being a sponsor is often a thankless job. You put your heart and soul into another person's recovery just to be let down. For every victory there are numerous setbacks and failures. It would be terrible if those successes didn't make everything worthwhile.

Always remember that the day will come when it's your turn to be the sponsor. Embody the principle of ehwaz and transport your folk to a higher state of consciousness.

Mannaz (man-noz)

Symbolizes: Rig ~ Ideal Man ~ Initiate

Mannaz is the totality of all that it means to be human. It is the inherent endowments of memory, fancy, and will (natural law), the teachings of Rig (philosophy), and our yearning for the Divine (mysticism). It is the rune of the ideal European man, a goal we should all strive for.

In the Rigsthula, Heimdall traveled to Midgard under the guise of Skef. He was taken in by the inhabitants of Aurvangaland, the progenitors of the Teutonic people. He taught them many things such as arts and crafts, agriculture and science. But most importantly he taught them how to worship the Goðin and how to live amongst each other in honesty and love. From the distillation of his teachings we get the Nine Noble Virtues and the Runlog.

During his time in Midgard, Heimdall also established the three classes of men: The Thrall (slave), the Karl (freeman), and the Jarl (chieftain). Although the classes were endowed with different capacities and gifts, the lore makes it clear that they are meant to work together as Heimdall's Holy Children.

When Heimdall was on his deathbed, he gathered his children to him and asked to be carried to the water. I like the Asatru Edda's version of his last words (originally from The Meditative Paradigms of Seidr):

Some transformed, he said, through time, some in the lust of combat, then released; some transformed by kindred minds blended to Powers, and, "I transform through you. Though I die many times to be with you. Some for power, some for perfection, some for their amber sheen, but I transform that you transform, as darts against the gathering gloom. Once I was bended at care", said Rigr-Heimdallr, "then let it go in my best bow's release. In my quietest stealth and bravest position, took the field of valor. While others held the shield, I

119

held also held sword."

To me, this passage describes the different ways people find meaning. The example Heimdall sets is that giving selfless service to your people is one way to find godly purpose in life.

In order to understand how this story relates to drug addiction, let us take a closer look at the three classes of men. Forget for a moment that our ancestors did believe in a caste system based on blood and lineage. What else separates the different classes from each other? The answer is influence. A thrall's circle of influence doesn't extend farther than himself and whatever pigpen he's mucking out. He focuses on the immediate concerns of existence. The Karl is a step above this. In addition to himself, he is liable for his family, his friends, and his duties to his Jarl. With greater responsiblities comes greater freedom and the ability to influence the world around him. At the very top of the social hierarchy is Jarl. He is responsible for the welfare of everyone below him. But this also means he has much farther to fall.

Take an honest assessment of yourself. Where do you stand on this hierarchy? Are you only focused on yourself and your immediate pleasure? Have you traded in a pigpen for a crack pipe or a needle? Does your foresight extend as far as your next high? If so, then you're a thrall. Tighten the fuck up.

I leave you with a passage from the Runlog. "Be happy and free, enjoy life to its fullest, and allow others to do the same, but be temperate in pleasing the senses, and recognize that certain aspects of human nature must be denied."

Laguz (lah-gooz)

Symbolizes: Lake ~ Passage To & From Life ~ Vital Power

Laguz is a rune that encompasses life and power. Our power comes from being tru to the virtues and standards of the Goðin. To recognize our faults and addictions is to be tru. Only when we find this truth in ourselves can it extend to our families, friends and the earth we live on.

We must constantly and consciously strive toward great heights. We call this ascending. Becoming. It can be trying at times, but it's worth it, and as you grow you begin to realize that perseverance is key. Throughout the passages of life one must seek to shed his old life, to improve. This transition then naturally leads to right action, which is a part of the Six-Fold Goal.

To understand and to recognize your faults is a part of this passage. We keep seeking knowledge and wisdom. To harvest that knowledge and replant the seeds for future generations is our highest purpose.

We look upon Odin as the greatest example. Odin sacrificed himself to acquire great wisdom. So why can't we sacrifice in some way, to better Become, and live by the virtues for all to follow? To walk tall and proudly, setting childish ways aside. We should want to be a cut above the rest! But power will never just be handed to you. It demands right action, individually and collectively. We must never lose sight that each of us represents the whole.

This brings me back to my point of being tru to oneself. One must strive to be virtuous by way of deed, and as a consequence, others will see a better way for themselves. It is simply not enough to talk the talk. Our passage is worn by our footsteps. We know we are not perfect. We may fall along the way. Yet is it not our way to relentlessly persevere? Get up! Stand up in the face of adversity and a society that can be viciously hostile. This means to possess the first virtue, courage. We courageously face conflict at any cost. We do not follow, bow down, or conform to destructive forces we face with our addictions. What a disciplined mind it takes! Heil Odin, Týr, and Thor!

To be Ásafolk is to feel a connection to our kin and be naturally inclined to act on it. We pull our folk up and stand with them in good times and bad. This connection brings us to a place where we will give support physically, spiritually, and materially to our kinsmen and kinswomen. In order to do this we employ the noble virtues of hospitality, loyalty, and honor. We should strive to live not just for ourselves, but for the greater cause; folk, family, and future!

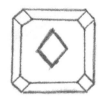

Ingwaz (ing-vaz)

Symbolizes: Seed ~ Potential Energy ~ Gestation ~ Frey

The rune Ingwaz has many different meanings. It is the seed that undergoes a gestation period, the genetic material passed down from generation to generation, or stored energy waiting to be released. It also symbolizes Ingvi-Frey which is the aspect I'm going to focus on in regards to drug addiction.

Frey and his sister Freyja are Vanir, but were adopted into Asgard when their father Njord was exchanged as a hostage. Frey rules over Alfheim and the Grotti-Mill, and controls all the processes of nature. He's one to invoke for fertility and abundance.

It's said that Frey will never make a woman weep, but one woman in particular did a number on him. One of the most popular stories involving Frey was when he fell in love with the Jötun maid Gerdr, daughter of Ægir and Gullveig. When he gazed into Jötunheim and saw her, light seemed to pour from her skin. For days afterwards he felt a great lovesickness and could not sleep.

Eventually Frey's childhood friend Odr came to see what was wrong. Odr could see that there would be no talking sense to Frey, so he vowed to help him win the giantess. Riding on Slepnir, with the mighty sword Gambanteinn at his side, Odr went to Jötunheim to ask Gerdr to marry his friend. At first he tried to bribe her with golden apples and Draupnir, and when that failed to work, he threatened to kill her and her family. For some reason the threats worked and Gerdr agreed to meet Frey in the Barri Grove.

Unbeknownst to Frey, the reason Gerdr had become so enticing to him was because Gullveig had enchanted her with seiðr. Gullveig's intentions were to trick Frey into giving up his invaluable sword Gambanteinn. It was a sword crafted by Volundr to fight Jötnar. If a Jötun tried to use it, the sword would kill the wielder and the Jötun race.

The Jötnar obviously wanted to get this terrible weapon from their foes. So Ægir asked for the sword as his daughter's bride price. Frey willingly gave up his most treasured possession, even though it meant that he would be under-equipped at Ragnarok. Frey will only have a stag horn at the last battle and Surtr will slay him with Gambanteinn.

When reading this story it's normal to focus on Frey and his all-encompassing love for Gerdr. She was his addiction, something he couldn't do without. But I want to approach things from a different angle; the point of view of the other Goðin.

Imagine how the Goðin must have felt to see Frey make this terrible mistake. Njord had to sit back and watch his son marry into the family of one of their oldest enemies. Odr had to put himself in danger traveling to Jötunheim. Worst of all, Odin and Frigga, who are able to foresee the events of Ragnarok, had to know that this marriage would ultimately lead to Frey's death and the destruction of Midgard.

Anyone who has had to watch a close friend or family member suffer from addiction can relate to this story. It kills you to see them destroying themselves. You want to shake them until they understand the stupidity of their decisions. You search for the words that can break the hold that drugs have over them. Their self-centeredness knows no bounds, and you alternate between pity and contempt for them. But in the end, if your wyrd is intertwined with this person, then you have no choice but to support them and continue to try to get them to seek help. Loyalty demands that we don't turn our backs on a family member or friend, no matter what.

Dagaz (da-gaz)

Symbolizes: Day ~ Polarity ~ Awakening

A new day dawning, the bright light of consciousness awakening to new possibilities; this is what Dagaz symbolizes.

Often when it comes to drug recovery, we place the focus on the most urgent part of addiction, the using and withdrawing. Not enough emphasis is placed on what happens after the worst part is over and you're facing a life of sobriety.

Just like walking out of a pitch black room into the light of day, the transition from addiction to sobriety can be jarring. Believe it or not, this can actually be the most dangerous time for an addict. This is because many addicts use drugs to escape from deeper psychological problems. Being confronted with these underlying issues when already reeling from heavy stress and sleep deprivation can make these problems seem even worse.

Doctors have long understood that improvements in a patient can be dangerous. Severe depression is characterized by hopelessness. The will to live is gone, yet paradoxically, the depressed person lacks the energy for suicide. The sad irony is, once there's some improvement in their condition, that's when they get the motivation to kill themselves. That is why, for a long time, antidepressants were thought to lead to suicide.

The psychological problems a recovering addict may be forced to deal with are varied. They could be repressed memories of physical or mental abuse, deep feelings of inferiority, or a profound sense of ennui, that nothing in life matters. Some problems you may be able to work out yourself. Exercise and proper sleep and nutrition will go a long way towards clearing things up. But for the more serious issues you may need to consult a doctor or therapist. If at any point you seriously contemplate suicide, seek help immediately.

While still getting accustomed to sobriety, you shouldn't make any other life-altering decisions. This isn't the time to switch jobs, enter a new relationship, or try to drop 20 pounds. All your energy should be directed at staying clean.

But there will come a day when dagaz shines in your life, and you realize that, while the urge to use drugs is still there and always will be, it has receded into the background. Once again you have room in your life for other things. This may be scary to some people who have forgotten what it means to have fun without drugs. It may even take a conscious effort to come up with healthy alternatives to getting high. This is a good time to make a Bucket List of things you want to do before you die. Start off with some of your easier goals, especially those that get you out and around other people. Here are a few possible examples to get you started:

- Take your kids to the beach, a park, or let them pick somewhere they want to go.
- Go hiking or camping in a nearby state park.
- Charter a boat with your buddies for a day of deep sea fishing.
- Start a heathen softball team and find some church teams to whoop up on.
- Organize a heathen weightlifting or crossfit competition.
- Stay in with your old lady, order takeout, and binge-watch whatever dumb movies she likes. Hey, at least it'll make her happy.

It may take some time for you to be able to enjoy the little things in life. But take the word of someone who's serving thirty years in prison; it's these little things you truly miss when they're gone. May the light of Dagaz shine on you.

Othala (oh-thah-la)

Symbolizes: Inheritance ~ Ancestral
Property ~ Sacred Enclosure

The primary aspect of Othala to consider in the paradigm of addiction recovery is its aspect of ancestral property, both in a literal and metaphorical sense.

The literal sense: Bluntly, if you live as a strung-out hippie, getting by just enough to get high, what will you ever be able to leave behind for the future? Though the "Ancestral Property" aspect is often taken to be one's DNA, there is a worldly meaning also. If you trade away wealth that could serve your folk for nothing more than a feeling, what sort of person are you?

How does your behavior change you in a way literal enough to be passed on to your heirs? The inheritance of a proclivity toward addiction is not fully understood, but all evidence points toward inheritance as a factor. There is a very real possibility that your self-indulgence could become the root of an undeniable, literal, ancestral curse. Consider the image of a newborn baby convulsing from heroin withdrawal and ask yourself if that is how you want your child's life to begin.

Less common aspects to consider:

Othala is a representation of Odin, in the AllFather aspect. This is an aspect of Oneness; being all things. Often, addiction is a mechanism to cover or suppress some portion of oneself. A major key to permanently beating addiction is to discover this disharmonious aspect and either change it or accept it, and bring it into the Whole. Only you can decide which.

Again, representing Odin, is the aspect of the Seeker for wisdom. Recovery is Becoming, plain and simple, and Becoming is not about being given answers, but finding the right questions.

- Where will the path you are on take you?
- What will you leave behind?

- What portion of your potential is this life unlocking for you?
- Do you believe that your everyday choices not only affect your orlog, but that they create literal changes within you that may adversely affect your offspring?
- What drives you to use drugs?

A further, less common aspect to consider is the position of Othala at the end of the third Ætt. In a sense, this in itself is representative of ending.

No beginning can come without an ending, so ask yourself, "What is my 'exit strategy' from addiction?"

Remember that the age of Baldr only comes after Ragnarok; a massive, catastrophic upheaval of the entire universe, not a gradual weaning away of the undesirable. Surtr and his minions are not to be wished away or just gradually pushed, but fought to a standstill and beaten back!

Steve's Saga

I've tried to get clean many times, for many different reasons. I've been given ultimatums by more than one probation officer, been faced with distraught family, disowned, evicted, lived homeless, locked up many times, and been through countless types of hell. And each time after the fog had cleared from my brain, and I could once again think clearly, I would tell myself the same thing: "This time I'm done."

At the time I would even sincerely mean it. I would have every intention of staying clean. But in the back of my head I would hold on to reservations. "Maybe I can get high just once in a while." Inevitably, I would get out and start doing well, get a job, a place, and a girl, and I would convince myself that I deserved a reward. So I would go get a little dope. A one time thing would turn into an only on the weekend thing, to an every day thing, and the cycle would start over again.

The time I was sitting in jail, realizing the gravity of my actions, facing nine indictments, I realized that I had made two major mistakes. The first one was that I had never tried to get clean because I wanted to. I had always tried to do it for, or at the demand of, someone else. During one of my attempts at sobriety, I actually accrued a little over a year of clean time. I was attending Narcotics Anonymous meetings regularly and had sponsored a couple of guys who were new to the program. I was so proud of these guys, and also proud of myself for being a part of their sobriety. It got to the point where they became my reason to stay clean. I couldn't tell these guys not to relapse and then do it myself. How would that look to them? Their sobriety depended on mine, didn't it?

Little did I know that just the opposite was true. Not long after I sponsored them, one of them relapsed. It was a crushing blow to me, in particular my ego. All of my work had meant nothing. This kid was right back at where he started, and I hadn't been able to do anything to stop it. This event led to one of my worst relapses, and ultimately, my first prison sentence.

I have since realized how much of a mistake it was to pin the hope of my recovery onto the success of another's. If you are going to get clean, you have to do it for you, and no other reason. You have to be selfish in the extreme when guarding your sobriety. There is a saying in the rooms of AA and NA, "Whatever you put before your recovery, you will lose," and it is very true. Your recovery must come first in your life, before family, friends, or anything, because without your sobriety, you are useless to everyone around you. I came to see that if I did the right thing, and walked as a Tru man should, those around me would take notice. And just as I fed off their natural positivity, they would feed off mine.

The second lesson I learned was that I could no longer hold on to reservations. I couldn't get high anymore. **Period**. And honestly, once I had truly become resolved to this, it wasn't that big of a deal. Sure, I've had some good times while using, but they have been far outweighed by the bad. Carl Von Clausewitz once said, "To introduce into the art of war the concept of moderation is an absurdity." And war is exactly what recovery is. It is a war against your addiction, against the countless demons each one of us carries within. It's a war against the thurses in the world who are constantly trying to disrupt our lives. In order to be successful you have to commit one hundred percent to this war. In all reality this is a fight to see who controls your life- you, or the drugs. We are all highly independently minded individuals who can't stand the thought of someone or something other than ourselves being in control of our thoughts and actions. I'm not saying it's going to be easy. The Goðin know my journey hasn't been and I haven't been perfect. I've made mistakes and stumbled along the way. But with each mistake I've learned something new about myself, and I've been able to apply these lessons to my life. Slowly I'm becoming a man that I can be proud of.

Steve, 2267

Hrafn's Saga

You know, I look at the people around me in prison and I can see why they're in here. Their lives were shaped by abuse and drug addiction and a lack of role models. It's harder for me to understand why I'm in here. I can't point to any of those reasons as the cause for my actions. All the mistakes I've made were due to my own pride, stupidity, and addiction.

I come from a good family. My mom taught me to be respectful,

130

spiritual, and to love learning. My dad taught me to stand up for myself, to keep my word, and to work hard. Everything good about me is because of them.

That's not to say my childhood was perfect. My dad was strict and whipped my ass often. I probably deserved the majority of the ass whippings and looking back, my life would have probably turned out better if he'd been around to discipline me longer. He left my mom when I was fifteen. My mom couldn't control me, and by the time I was sixteen I was living on my own in a party house.

But not all of my family's lessons stuck with me. I've never had much respect for the law. I viewed laws as obstacles to work around in order to make a dollar. When I was fifteen, I copped my first ounce of pot, and by the time I finished high school I was selling fifteen to twenty pounds a week.

I loved everything about the lifestyle: The money of course, and being able to afford things I'd only dreamed of when growing up in Section 8 housing. I loved partying with women who would've never looked twice at me if I worked fast food. I loved walking into hotel parties at the Oceanfront and knowing everyone was waiting for me to get there. But most of all I loved the excitement of relying on my own wits, knowing that one wrong move could end up with me getting robbed or locked up. High school was boring in comparison but I somehow still managed to graduate with honors.

I mention partying, but at this point in my life the partying was nowhere near what it would one day become. Pot made me self conscious and paranoid. The one time I did coke, I didn't feel anything (although that wouldn't always be the case). My first experience with opiates was a blessing and a curse. This hot chick at a party popped an 80 milligram Oxy in my mouth when I was shitfaced drunk. I thought it was an E pill and it almost killed me. But I say in the long run it was a blessing because it turned me off from opiates to this very day.

My drugs of choice were Adderal and alcohol. The Adderal could keep me up for days of hustling. It also helped sober me up when I was too drunk. I was drunk most of the time. I loved alcohol. It helped curb my anxiety and made me feel like I belonged. The problem was, I could never get the hang of social drinking. I only drank to get wasted, and when I got wasted I liked to fight. I would go from 140 pounds to 240 pounds after three shots. It made me feel good to be known as the type of guy who didn't give a fuck, but looking back I see it was a false type of courage.

I always told myself that only three things would make me change my ways and quit selling drugs: death, prison or a child. But back then I was invincible, too smart to get caught, and always used protection. Those things only happened to other people. Did I mention I was smart?

Yeah, well, what happened next reminds me of the part in Blow where I always turn the movie off, when he's partying in Mexico right before his life turns into a shit show. That's what happened to me. One of my friends set me up and I caught a trafficking and concealed weapon charge. The cops raided my grandma's house, my truck, and my boat. Luckily I hadn't registered either so it was an unlawful search and the five pounds they found were inadmissible. If you think this means they gave them back you'd be wrong. I ended up wearing the distribution and weapon charge and had to pay for my bond, my lawyer, fines, and pretrial release. Then I found out that drug offenders are ineligible for college financial aid, so I had to pay for my own tuition.

But at least I was still smart. Now I had to sell drugs just to get back on top. Then once I got back on top, I had to sell drugs to make up for lost time. This brings me to one of my biggest downfalls: I'm just smart enough to be really fucking stupid. I can rationalize almost anything and make it sound good. Living as an Ásatrúar has helped me in that regard. I now have a moral frame of reference that makes sense to me.

The next few years were a slow but steady slide into the penitentiary. There's no need to go into detail, so I'll just hit the lowlights...

- I started partying with strippers who really liked coke. Pretty soon I really liked coke, too.
- I cheated on and mentally skull-fucked the only woman I ever really loved. She transferred from UNC to be with me and I made sure she regretted it.
- I bought a pistol. It started as a fashion accessory, but the grimy, wannabe gangsters I was hanging around made it so I eventually needed it.

- I slept in my car with my dog and a pocketful of cash many nights. Ironically, it's easier to buy a gun than it is to rent an apartment.
- I got so wasted I barely remember my sister's graduation or my dad's wedding. Then I ruined my mom's perfect Christmas by passing out on the floor and waking up and trying to fight my cousins.
- One of my childhood friends got shot during a deal. Another caught a trafficking charge carrying my drugs.
- I shot a guy during a three day, sleep deprived coke, tequila, and Xanax binge.

Because of that last one I'm sitting in prison, serving a 33 year sentence. You'd think I'd feel remorse for it, but I don't. Would I have done things differently if I could go back in time? Of course, but that's not an option that any of us have, so I have to accept the wyrd that the Norns have laid for me. To be honest, the things I regret are much worse. I regret all the times I let my family down. I regret turning people on to their first hit of coke and making thralls of my Folk. I regret all the beautiful women I degraded and treated like whores, instead of the potential mothers that they are. When I die and go to my Helthing, these are the nids I feel I will be called upon to answer for, not the death of some junkie. Drugs are what led me down that path, and that's why I wrote this book, to help someone before they make the serious mistakes that I did.

Hrafn Rekkr

Stacy's Saga

Everyone who calls himself an Ásatrúar or an Odinist should be familiar with the story of Ragnarok. The story starts with Fjalarr retrieving Gambanteinn for Surtr. Then the Gullinkambi awakens the Einherjar and Odin. Finally, that soot-red cock crows in the underworld. Everyone is prepared for battle. The Earth shakes to its very core, trees are loosened, mountains fall, and all the fetters sever and break. Loki and the Fenris-wolf are freed. Skoll captures Sol and offers her to Fenris, who swallows her. All is dark. The stars disappear from the Heavens and mankind thinks it has suffered a terrible disaster. This is just the beginning of the story. However, this is the exact point at which my story begins. I do not truly know if there ever was light in my life, but there sure was darkness...

As a kid, my life seemed pretty normal on the surface. We had a nice house with a pool in the backyard. Both of my parents were happily married. I have an older sister who was adopted and an identical twin brother. My father worked for Norfolk Southern Railroad. My mother stayed at home to take care of us kids. Like I said, all was well on the surface. However, behind closed doors was a different story. My parents were very abusive drug addicts who ran around with the Renegade Bikers in Norfolk, VA. back in the 80's. We took beatings that no kid should ever have to endure, for a list of reasons ranging from, "For the hell of it," to back talking, to bad school grades, to not doing our chores up to par. It was so bad at one point, when I was in third grade, all of us kids were taken from my parents and placed in foster homes. Of course back in the 80's it was hard to prove child abuse and my parents were given back custody after a lengthy court battle. Back then, with the right amount of money and the right attorney, anything could be swept under the rug. About a year later, my father was arrested on a number of charges ranging from "distribution of cocaine" to "weapons charges," when the DEA and ATF kicked our house in. The cops took us kids to a neighbor's house where we watched our house being ransacked and my father carted off to jail. Somehow he paid his way out from under it all by hiring Pete Decker (anyone from Tidewater knows who he is) and he walked. The 80's were funny like that. In the process of it all, we lost our house, our cars, and were seriously in debt. So we moved to VA Beach for a fresh start. (I only shared that part of the story with you so you would know how dysfunctional my life was from the start.)

We moved to Pembroke/Aragona and things settled down a bit, but not too much. My parents were still abusing drugs and us. That's just how life was back then. I thought all kids went through that same bullshit. When I was about 8 years old my sister snuck into my parents room and stole some roaches out of the ashtray and some crazy looking ceramic bong. I took my first bong-hit. I remember feeling as if I were in a dream. Everything seemed all fuzzy and super slow. I was hungry as hell, too. I ate a whole jar of marshmallow cream, then I puked it all up. (Good times, right?) Anyways, that was my first experience with drugs and I couldn't wait to do it again. After that day I used to stand by my sister's bedroom door and wait to hear her cough so I could bust into her room and catch her doing bong-hits and threaten to tell my parents if she didn't share.

A few years after that my brother and I would stay the weekend with a friend of ours because we had this tree-fort in his back yard that we hung out in while his mom threw parties for her biker friends. We used to sneak back into the house and steal beers or sometimes her biker friends would give them to us. I guess they thought it was cool to get little kids drunk? It is what it is…. I though it was cool, too. Life was pretty much a blur of pot smoke and beer until I was 13 years old.

When I was 13 years old my father suffered a stroke in his sleep. I remember getting up for school that morning and thinking it was weird that he was still in bed instead of at work. Off to school I went. A couple hours later I was called to the principal's office and told that my father was in critical condition at Bayside Hospital. When we got to the hospital he was hooked up to life support. They said he would be a vegetable for the rest of his life or we could pull the plug. My mother chose to pull the plug. We all said our good-byes. Afterwards, I sat outside the hospital with my brother smoking a cigarette, having a conversation about how at least we wouldn't get beat on anymore. That's a crazy way to feel over your father's death. But he was a very mean person with a dark soul.

Shortly after his death my mother received a huge life insurance check. Plus she received his railroad retirement fund and a check for my brother and I of $1500 a month. She also received $1100 a month. We were set. My mother did not have to work. Losing my father was a tough break for my mother. She suffered a nervous breakdown. After that it seemed as if she just gave up. She started smoking crack heavily. She blew through all that money within a year's time. Luckily we still had our monthly checks. My mother would disappear on her "crack binges" for days or sometimes weeks. She would reappear as if nothing had happened. She'd shower, eat, and then sleep for days. At this point my sister was out of the house, married, with a kid of her own. Needless to say, my house became the neighborhood party house. My mother didn't care about anything except where her next hit came from. My weekly allowance as a teenager became a quarter ounce of pot. My mother would also buy beer for everyone to drink.

Around his time I tried my first hit of LSD and had acid parties at my house. If you wanted to party, my house was where you did it. My brother and I started to sell pot, acid, cocaine and anything else we could get our hands on. Of course we all know how things continued to progress. It was a downward spiral. I started to sell crack cocaine to everyone I knew. Before long, everyone was strung out. One day I was bagging up my crack and my mother walked in and caught us. I thought I was in big trouble. Instead all she wanted was a blast. So we loaded her up, only to have her tell us that our stuff sucked and to go get rid of it and bring the money home. When I came home my mom's friend was there. This dude showed me how to cook crack with test tubes and ammonia. For real, dude was my best coke connect up until I got incarcerated on this bid. I ended up dropping out of school because it interfered with selling drugs. Before I knew what happened I had a full fledged crack house and was smoking crack with my mother every day. Shortly after that I had burned all my bridges so I resorted to robbing drug dealers and stores to support my growing taste for crack cocaine. I found myself on the run for a couple of the robberies. It wasn't long before I was caught and sent to Tidewater Detention Home. I got certified as an adult. I made bond and back to Aragona I headed. I continued in my usual antics. When my time came I went to court and the judge sentenced me to serve 14 years in prison with 6 suspended. My mother did not bother to contest me being certified as an adult, nor did she hire me an attorney. I guess it just got easier if I weren't around?

I made it to Southampton Corr. Center when I had just turned 17 years old and prison was crazy. I smoked pot and drank hooch almost every day. You couldn't tell me shit back then (still can't). I was young. I was violent. I was racist as hell and I really didn't give a shit who didn't like it. I stayed at SHCC for four years. The very day they opened Lawrenceville Corr. Center I was transferred there. If you think LVCC is wide open now, then you don't have a clue. I was the very first person to get on with an oz. of pot there. I hustled on the yard day and night. Shortly after arriving there I was reintroduced to crack. It wasn't long after that I did my first shot of heroin. I was in love from the first shot. Every crack I had in my soul from a fucked up childhood was filled. All the missing pieces fit back together. I found what I was missing. I got into a lot of trouble at LVCC. I caught two assault cases on the CO's and was shipped to Nottoway. This was back when DOC changed from A,B,C custody to levels 1-6. Nottoway was level 4. I continued to abuse drugs at Nottoway. I stayed there for a year and then finally it was time to go home. I had pulled 7 1/2 years on an 8 year, old law sentence. I did my time the hard way to say the least.

While I was serving my time my twin brother was running around the country following the Grateful Dead, Phish, Widespread Panic, and going to music festivals. So it only seemed right that I follow suit. Pretty much as soon as I got out of prison we went on tour. This was a whole new experience for me. Life was amazing and full of adventure. We crisscrossed all over the country, from city to city, show to show, trafficking whatever drugs we could get our hands on. Mostly ecstasy and LSD, but we would sell anything as long as we could turn a profit so that we had gas to get to the next show, a hotel room to sleep in, and food to eat. Its expensive living on the road like that. We called ourselves the G. D.F., better known as the "Grateful Dead Family." We took care of ours and I felt as if I finally found my place in life. It's a hard life living on the road like that. I basically shot dope everyday so I felt good enough to hustle in the hot sun and run around the parking lots of the different concert venues. I'm sure I copped dope in every major city across the country at some point. When summer tour ended, my brother was in prison for trafficking LSD. So I headed back to VA Beach with a monster habit. Needless to say you don't last on the streets of VA Beach with a habit. Once I had burned through all my money and burned my bridges, I resorted to stealing to support my growing heroin habit. I found myself back in jail with a violation, a forgery, and a grand larceny.

I was sentenced to serve 4 1/2 years. I did that sentence at Buckingham. I continued to abuse drugs every chance I got. When my time was up my friends picked me up at the back gate of Buckingham and they gave me a card with 500 inside it and two tickets to watch "The Dead" play at the Gorge, in Washington State. We drove for three days and barely made it to the show before the first set started. I never even reported to probation and parole in VA Beach. Needless to say, it was summertime, the Dead were in Tour, and I was back in my element. I continued in my drug addictions. The rest is history. I went back to prison for a third time. The one recurring theme in my life is that I've always used drugs and I always end up back in prison.

Now, at 41 years old, life seems to have passed me by. I'm currently serving my 5th prison sentence. This time I got 13 years for robbery. Right now I have around 4 years left. I lost my family this time. My old lady finally had enough. She was a soldier. I just pushed her away because it's hard to be there for someone when you're always in prison. I still talk to my stepdaughter, but both of my grandbabies don't even know me.

When I first got locked up I felt as if my life was over. I actually tried to commit suicide when I first got to St. Brides. I got a good name on the street back home and St. Brides is in my backyard. All my neighborhood drug dealers are there. I copped a rack of heroin, then I shot three fifties and went out. A friend of mine decided he wasn't gonna let me die on a pissy bathroom floor in prison, so he got me help. I woke up in the ambulance. I got clean for about a year and a 1/2. During that clean time my buddy Mike Ingram got me started down our ancestral path. We all got jammed up at St. Brides and shipped around the state for our beliefs. That's how I ended up here at Augusta Corr. Center. I met Wayne Hopkins here and he schooled me to Ásatrú. For those of you who know me, you know I still struggle with my addictions. Addiction is a disease. I'm sure I will battle those demons for the rest of my life. There is no magic switch to turn it off. I wish there was so I could turn it off. I recently took a class that explained how drug addictions rewire your brain. It was an eye-opener to say the least. Some people think it's a matter of choice. Willpower alone is not enough. Anyone who ever knew me, knows that my will is a force to be reckoned with. It takes serious lifestyle changes, self-examination, and honesty. But more than anything else you have to want the self destruction to end. If your motivation is for someone else, you will fail every time. That's my only promise to you. You also have to remember that even if you slip and fall, it's not the end of the road. Pick yourself up and brush the dirt off and try again. No body is perfect. Even the God's made mistakes. Now I know there are those of you reading this, saying to yourself, "Who does this junkie think he is?" If you only see me as a hypocrite, well then, I guess you missed my point. I only share my story with you so you know that you are not alone in your struggles. We all battle the same demons. I cannot tell you to do as I have done. Believe me, I am all fucked up. Instead I tell you to seek what I seek. Search for the light. It's in you. I leave the same lessons the Goðin left with us when they battled at Ragnarok.

Odin goes into battle against the Fenris-wolf. Thor goes against the Midgard serpent. Týr fights against Hati. Once Odin is swallowed by the wolf, Vidarr avenges him by ripping open the wolf's jaws, stabbing him through his heart. Heimdall battles with Loki and they kill each other. The Midgard Serpent and the Fenris-Wolf are spawns of Loki and Gullveig. Gullveig is the witch who brings seiðr (sorcery) into the world. Loki represents the "Destroying Fire" that constantly burns in the world. So it's perfect that the serpent and the wolf represent the destructive forces that constantly try to consume us. Odin (our wisdom), Týr (our sense of right and wrong) and Thor (our strength), battle against the "original destroyers." Frey battles Surtr (the internal fire) and falls. Surt then burns Midgard (yourself) until the whole world is charred and sinks into the sea. The stars fall from the heavens and Yggdrasil is consumed by flames that leap toward the heavens.

This event is a necessary part in the grand scheme of things because a second time the Earth will rise up from the sea and all will be beautiful. Lif (Life) and Lifthrasir (Yearning for Life), hide themselves in the Odainsakr (the Acre if Immortality). From these two the world will once again be inhabited. The Æsir meet on Idavollr, where they speak of the World Tree, each reminded of their own orlog, and Odin's ancient runar, remembering the mysteries revealed to each of them and the serpent and the wolf. Each never forgetting the lessons learned along the way. Vidarr (Far ruler) and Valid (Warrior) return, along with Thor's sons Magni (the Strong) and Modi (the Courageous) who possess Mjöllnir (the Crusher). Baldr (the Light) returns with Hodr (the Battle Warrior) to reside in Valholl (the Hall of the Chosen). Sol bore a daughter before she was swallowed by the wolf. She rides her mother's course across the sky, providing us with nourishing light. There is a hall called Gimle (the Fire Shelter) where the virtuous multitudes dwell. Happiness is enjoyed forever. Odin (Our Wisdom) returns to settle strife and sit in judgement, laying down the laws that will last forever.

Knowing what we all know from the Eddas and our personal battles with the forces that try to destroy us all. With Goðin that reside within us all, whose names represent a wide variety of things such as wisdom, strength, or sense of right and wrong, the light and battle warrior, just to name a few. Armed with weapons like Mjöllnir "the Crusher", I ask you again....do you seek what I seek? Find the light that exists within us all. Hold onto it. Do not fret if you stumble along the path. The Goðin also did. Pick yourself up and find the strength to seek what I seek and shine your light so that others may see when they lose their way...

Stacy Lee Sawyer

Gumby's Saga

Heroin took everything from me. It took my money, it took my health, it took my innocence... It even took my good name. But more than that it took the life of someone I love. Someone who irrevocably changed me forever. Her name was Jessica Richmond. Kids on lot called her Hatter; I called her Mama Bear. This is my story of what being a heroin addict was like for me.

My name is Gumby, and I love to get high. Always have, always will. For many years I was successful at not allowing my drug use to interfere with other aspects of my life. That is, until I met Hatter. She changed everything. We hooked up during Dead Tour '09, and the whole time I knew she was a junkie. I also knew she would slowly pull me down with her if I didn't get away, but I still chose to stay with her. So really, I drug myself down. She didn't want that life for me but I guess I was so blinded by love that I couldn't see what I was getting into. I was young and thought I could save her, but in the end I became just as lost as she ever was.

After the summer RatDog tour of '09, we moved back to California to trim nuggs on a friend's farm. Heroin on the West Coast is hella cheap, and it wasn't long before we both developed serious habits. After we ran out of trim work we decided to go pick mushrooms in Oregon, and on our way back we wrecked our Jeep. Totalled that fucker on a mountain just north of Crescent City. We spent the next several weeks with a couple of tweakers who were supposedly trying to head south in their motorhome, but because their entire existence revolved solely around cooking meth, we didn't make it very far. We ended up parting ways on not so good terms and hitched a ride to People's Park in Berkeley. We camped in the park at night and flew signs during the day, making just enough money to buy small amounts of black tar heroin. During our time with the tweakers I had learned to cook meth and before long I reverted to that as my main source of income.

One night, Hatter and I ate some acid and got into an argument over heroin. I told her if she didn't shut up I'd stab her in the neck with a needle full of sulfuric acid. She did not respond well. She called 6up and they chased my dumbass all across Berkeley until I finally gave up. They realized I was spun and 51-50'd me in a San Mateo psych ward for 72 hours. Trust me, that shit sucked! Once I got out I headed back to Berkeley to find out that Hatter had gone to San Francisco to stay with an Indian kid named Raj that we had sold some L to on the Haight a while back. I never should have contacted her again after she had me locked up, but she had all my shit and I needed it back. So I headed to the city and we made up. We stayed with Raj for awhile, until he got tired of us constantly shooting dope in his 3,000 dollar a month sky rise apartment and kicked us out.

We then made our way back up the Haight and crashed in the Panhandle and Golden Gate Park. We had no house, no car, and very little money. We became street cats who did whatever we needed to do in order to support our habits. I custied the shit out of tourists, selling 80 dollar 10 strips, and 60 dollar eighths of nuggs. It quickly got to the point where I stopped being able to pay my bills, so I simply stopped trying. I ripped off a lot of good kids in order to maintain my addiction. I broke just about every moral code in the book and am utterly ashamed by it. I turned into the worst of the worst... using my good name in order to rip kids off. They trusted me because they knew I was Family, and I took full advantage of that. I didn't have room in my life anymore for anything other than heroin. It completely consumed me. I was absolutely convinced I'd die in that city with a needle in my arm, and even though I knew all that I still couldn't stop.

I flew signs and sold drugs on the Haight with Hatter for almost 2 years before I finally left. Hatter didn't even leave with me. I never gave her the chance. I knew she was selling herself for dope, and even though I loved her I knew we were over and that I had lost her to heroin. She put me through so much shit... She stole a Hell's Angel's wallet and pinned it on me. Luckily, he's my first cousin. She sold fake L on the Haight and put my name and word on it. She cheated on me, lied, and stole from me whenever she could. We had loved one another deeply, but we had become so strung out that we could never fix all the broken shit between us. We kept hurting each other because of dope. I know she only did those things because of our habits. I know she loved me, and I know she was scared of what we had become.

She bought me a ring that had an inscription in it that read "Serva me, Serva bote". That is Latin for "Save me, I'll save you". She didn't know that when she got it, and we didn't know how prophetic that inscription truly was. In the end I couldn't save her. I barely saved myself. I left one morning out of the blue and never said a word to her. That is something I will always regret, and I'll have to live with for the rest of my life. I stranded her in that city. I left a lost girl all alone in a city filled with broken promises and disease. I did that... Nobody else. Just me. She told me before that she couldn't survive that place without me, and I think that was why I had stayed for so long. I loved her more than I'd ever loved anyone and I couldn't stand the thought of losing her. We were both lost, but at least we were lost together.

She's gone now and she haunts my dreams. I see her in them sometimes, passing me in the streets of San Francisco. I'll never completely forgive myself for leaving her, but I hope that one day I can find peace. Since then, I've gotten myself busted for smiling on a cloudy day. I had left San Francisco to get clean, yet ended up in prison for making drugs to sell so that I could continue the very habit I was running from! I ended up with a nine and a half year prison sentence that most likely saved my life. I am one of the lucky ones. I survived a full blown heroin addiction. Hatter was not so lucky, and there's not a day that goes by where I don't think of her. My time in San Francisco broke my heart, and I don't know if I could ever go back again. I'm scared to death of the memories I left there. Those were the darkest days of my entire existence, and I relive them in some way everyday. I see her face in my dreams, and hear her voice in the wind. I miss her more than I could ever describe, and I want her to know I'm sorry and that I love her…

So yeah, to me, being a heroin addict meant losing all that I ever wanted in life. It meant being every single thing that I stood against. It meant losing a part of my soul that I'll never get back. It meant waiting in line at the needle exchange every Wednesday to get a new box of 100 needles, just to run out again by Saturday. It meant watching the girl I love destroy her body, and letting her get used and abused by filthy men, just so we could have drug money. It meant giving up on ever seeing my daughter again. It meant overdosing in shitty dope den hotels, abscesses and blown out veins. It meant surviving solely on sloppy second kick downs and the free PB and J sandwiches that the HOT (Homeless Outreach Team) passed out. It meant sleeping in the street at night, and hustling tourists during the day. It meant making meth in the People's Park female bathroom in broad fucking daylight! It meant hardly ever eating, and **never** taking care of myself. It meant letting my teeth go to shit. It meant not giving a flying fuck about anyone or anything other than getting dope, and which Walgreens was still open at 3 AM so that I could buy a fifty cent needle. It meant losing everything we owned over and over again in different hotels because we couldn't pay our rent. It meant being the scum of the earth… It meant all of those things and much, much more.

It had all started off as just fun and games. Us getting high and having a good time. But getting high became getting well, and getting well meant becoming someone I never thought I could be… Anyways, this is my story. I hope it will inspire you to make better choices than I did. Much love and respect.

Gumby, 2267

Bear's Saga

When most people think of the words addict or addiction, they think of a drug abuser or a junkie. Also, someone who cannot control their impulses, and relapse to whatever they are addicted to. It's true that drugs are powerfully addictive. But for me, it wasn't so much the drugs themselves as it was the lifestyle that came with it.

What I mean by that is exactly what it sounds like, the money I made, the girls, the bar, the strip club, and the club scene. The option of being able to do what I want, when I wanted. I mean, I could have a pocketful of money and it was never enough. It went from doing what I had to do, to enjoying what I was doing. While I was living life up, I was helping to tear people's lives down. I was literally spending 500/weekend at bars, 700/week at nice restaurants, and 1,000/week on clothes and shoes. Not to mention daily and monthly spending (cigs, groceries, insurance, cell phone, bills). The whole time I would watch people scrape together what they could afford to spend with me to get their fix of coke or pills.

While I was living the luxurious fast life, I was helping to slowly tear apart people's lives. It wasn't until I actually sat down and thought about this that I realized I wasn't any better than the ones who were addicted to what I was providing for them. I wasn't just taking money from them, I was also taking from their kids, their parents, and their loved ones who were probably trying to help them. But at that time I didn't care. The money was fueling my lifestyle which I enjoyed and was addicted to.

Not only did I tear apart those lives, but I could never have a stable one for myself. Don't get me wrong: I enjoyed the bachelor's lifestyle, but when it was time to get serious with someone, how can you be serious? More than likely the two of you met while living that lifestyle. The late, late nights, the females always around (for whatever reason), the constant risk of getting locked up, robbed, or even worse. So how could you have a stable relationship when you aren't stable yourself? More than likely you only attract someone for your drugs, money, cars, or what you can materially offer them. While you can offer things everyone will be around; when you have nothing to offer, you'll see only the ones who matter are still there.

With all this being said, I just wanted to offer my input. It doesn't always have to be the drug itself that is the addiction, sometimes its the lifestyle that's the downfall, both to the user and the provider. It is easy to sit here now and point out the wrongs that we should or shouldn't do. But for those heading home or those who are already there, think about who all you will affect next time you want to rob, steal, or simply spend money that could be used to feed your family or doing something your kids will enjoy rather than your thirty minute high. Give people memories to hold on to rather than a lifetime full of regrets and doubt.

Randall "Bear" Hutchens

Báleygr's Saga

Heilsa. Everyone has a story. A story unique to them but still much the same. My name is Báleygr Gunnr. I am an addict, and this is just a part of my story.

There are a lot of misconceptions about women in the drug world. Labels I have to defend myself against, as if being in recovery isn't hard enough! You will not find war stories here. Nor will you find excuses. What you will find is my testimony of how our religion saved my life.

I come from a long line of extremely strong and gifted women. My bloodline is 84 percent Norse and the rest is a mix of places my ancestors invaded and stayed. I was raised in a Christian household. Questions I had never got real answers. I felt no "spiritual" attachments. I was empty, cold. Tragedies struck my life which left me angry and bitter towards this so called "loving god". When I first found recovery 20 years ago, everyone had a "Higher Power", except me. Was I doomed to failure because I couldn't pray to a God of my understanding? I had no religion. I was drawn to the organics of Wicca, but it didn't sit right at all. Seven and a half years ago the Goðin put some pretty powerful and knowledgeable brothers in my path. My awakening began. We women, who are tru, are warriors in our own rite. I knew I would be a minority in this way of life as well as a rarity, but my blood and ancestors called me. With an endless thirst, I read everything I could get my hands on regarding Odinism, Asatru, Wotanism, and Germanic Heathenry. I had a book called the "Rites of Odin" (forgive me the name of the author). Yes, it included the Nine Noble Virtues. Yes, it included the Rede of Honor. Most importantly it contained fairly strict absolutes as to how we should carry ourselves, and honor our Goðin by our examples. I came across a "rule" of how we should always be battle-ready, and for those who took to excess should NOT partake in opiates or mead! Ahh...

Opiates and mead. There it was in writing. Our ancestors knew in times of old that some would have problems. There it was! My absolute. I had dishonored my Goðin, my body, my mind, my family.

The next morning my life began again. Working out, running, healthy eating, studies. I was going to be an example of what a tru Aryan woman should be. Truly embrace the virtues. Understand the principles of our ancestors. This is a personal journey. We can learn so much in the literature. I had to tap into the heart of the ways of kith and kin. The Nine keep me strong and sane.

I've been told by a goði that mead during blot is okay. I swear I get sick every time! I honor and respect all aspects of our way of life. I am rare, I am tru, I am a shield maiden. I am the exception and the example. I hope my words have helped at least one person with perspective or have been looked upon as profound.

Fara Heil.

Nicole "Báleygr Gunnr"

Made in United States
Orlando, FL
06 November 2022

24256962R00085